A FIRESIDE BOOK

PUBLISHED BY

SIMON & SCHUSTER INC.

NEW YORK ■ LONDON

TORONTO ■ SYDNEY

TOKYO

DO THE RIGHT THING

A SPIKE LEE JOINT

SPIKE LEE WITH LISA JONES

PHOTOGRAPHY BY DAVID LEE

Fireside
Simon & Schuster Building
Rockefeller Center
1230 Avenue of the Americas
New York, New York 10020

FIRESIDE and colophon are registered trademarks
of Simon & Schuster Inc.

DESIGNED BY DIANE STEVENSON/SNAP-HAUS GRAPHICS

Manufactured in the United States of America

10 9 8 7 6 5 4 3 2 1

Library of Congress Cataloging in Publication Data

ISBN 0-671-68265-2

ACKNOWLEDGMENTS

Many thanks to Malaika Adero, my editor at Simon & Schuster, and to Cynthia Simmons, Monty Ross, Susan Fowler, and the staff of Forty Acres and a Mule Filmworks.

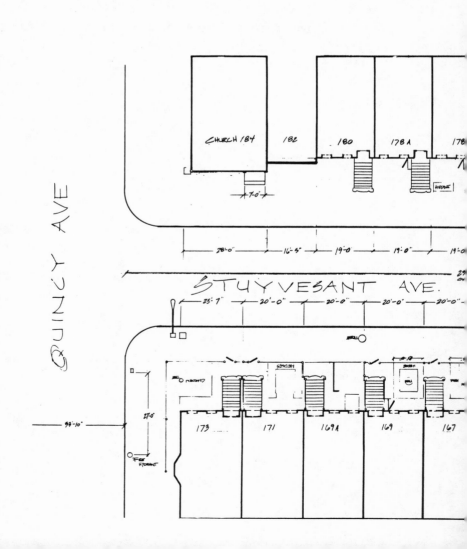

QUINCY AVE

CHURCH 184   182   180   178A   178

7-0"

28'-0"   16'-5"   19'-0"   19'-0"   19'-0"

STUYVESANT AVE.

25'-7"   20'-0"   20'-0"   20'-0"   20'-0"

27'-0"

93'-10"

FIRE HYDRANT

173   171   169A   169   167

DEDICATION

To the residents of Stuyvesant Street, between Quincy and Lexington, in the heart of Bed-Stuy, who put up with us for an entire summer.

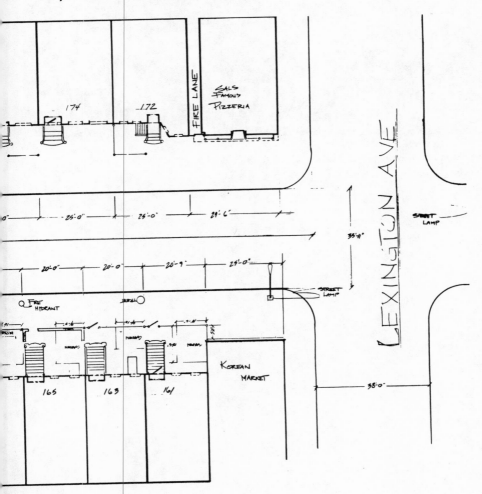

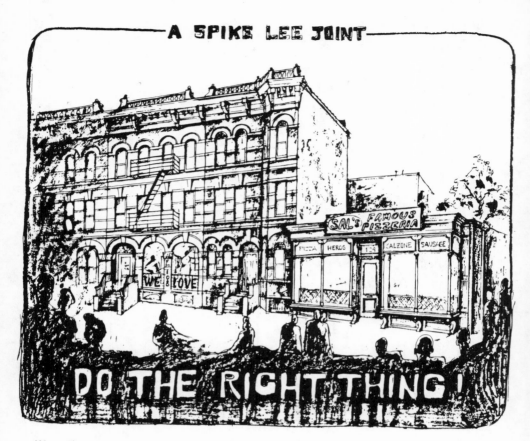

Wynn Thomas's original production sketch for Sal's Famous Pizzeria.

CONTENTS

FOREWORD

BROOKLYN ON MY MIND

When Spike Lee asked me to do the foreword for his book, I felt both honored and stupefied. Honored, because Lee is one of the most innovative and consistent auteurs of this decade—black, white, yellow, whatever. Stupefied, because I have never understood Brooklyn.

I'm from Harlem, the onetime capital of the Black world. Harlem's contribution to the arts, politics, religion, and glamour is well known. When I hear the word *Harlem*, it brings to mind Malcolm X and 125th Street in front of the Theresa Hotel, or James Brown playing to standing room only at the Apollo. When I think of Brooklyn, I scratch my head. I still get lost in the big B every time I step off the subway. Brooklyn is the urban Alpha Centauri to me.

My earliest recollections of Brooklyn are almost chimerical: a big sun that stretched across the sky like a piece of yellow Bazooka gum, heating brownstones and tenements to a brick-oven red; sidewalks that oozed metallic; and July air that pushed through hot iron grates every time the A train roared underneath.

As kids, my younger brother and I were treated to an annual Christmas expedition to Abraham & Straus on Fulton Street. We rode the A train with bated breath from 145th Street in Harlem, all the way to Jay Street–Borough Hall in Brooklyn. Once inside the store, we would pull our beleaguered mother to the seventh floor to bum-rush the toy department like Eliot Ness and Rico. Then we'd head for a tiny stand on Hoyt Street and eat the best kosher hot dogs in New York. As I bit into my third one—yes, I was down with the "husky" department at A&S—I knew Brooklyn was *it*.

I remember seeing the same guideposts in Brooklyn that I had seen in my native Harlem: fish-n'-chips and barbecue-rib joints, loud record shops with the local Blye-knit-and-sharkskin—draped Arthur Murrays demonstrating the Funky Broadway out in front, wash-n'-dry coin-o-mats, storefront churches, liquor stores, barbershops, numbers holes.

But the Brooklyn of my childhood was different from Harlem in the sense that its borders expanded far beyond the Lenox-to-Amsterdam Avenue, 110th-to-155th Street "boundaries" of Harlem. In Brooklyn, I seemed to see Black faces for miles and miles. If Harlem was the emotional capital of the world, then Brooklyn's Bedford-Stuyvesant, Fort Greene, Crown Heights, and Brownsville had to be our collective solar system.

Nineteen seventy-five. I hated Brooklyn. See, I fancied myself a ballplayer back then, and I played in a couple of tournaments. Let me say this: If I had the heart, I think I could have developed into a pretty good swing man.

There was only one thing wrong. Crowds unnerved me. Every time I walked to half-court, fear traveled down every limb of my body. And that's something you can't hide from a crowd. So you know when I played against this team called the Brooklyn Wildcats —who hailed from either Bed-Stuy or Da 'Ville—it was the beginning of the end of my b-ball career.

It was an elimination round for the City-wide Summer Tournament. I played for the Harlem . . . Whatevers. I've blocked out the name of my team, but I remember the guy's name who played center for the Wildcats: Sidney Green. About 6'5" and 215 pounds of muscle, Sidney plays for the New York Knicks now. Since I was the biggest kid on my team—at seventeen, a sliver under six feet—I was pitted against Sidney.

My man did an *Enter the Dragon* chop across my back as I got the step on him during a fast break, stuck me to the boards four times, stole the ball from me three times, and swatted two of my jumpers into the bleachers. Needless to say, my Harlem Whatevers were routed by the Wildcats. The final score was like 90 to 46. I scored four points, two of which came from the foul line. I had a problem with Brooklyn for a long time after that game.

It must not have been too much of a problem, though, because in 1977 I enrolled in Medgar Evers College on Carroll Street in Brooklyn. It was a station of higher learning, strange accents, and curious Black people. I call the Black Brooklyn natives I encountered during that time *curious* because they were different from any other Blacks I had known. For one thing, they were intellectuals, without wearing their IQs on their sleeves. I used to sit on Eastern Parkway smoking with the fellas and talking about how Claude McKay came up with the first "on-the-road" novel, *Banjo,* decades before Kerouac; whether Richard Wright's *Outsider* was a vivid tableau of existentialism or the greatest argument for man's need of an omniscient God; and which Rasta spot on President Street had the best cheeba.

Even women in Brooklyn were different. They were more independent than the women I had known, financially, sexually, and emotionally. Every day was Sadie Hawkins Day for Brooklyn. They didn't wait on the fellas. I remember this one young lady who invited me over to her house to join her and a girlfriend for a horizontal troika because "we haven't been 'done' in quite some time," as she calmly told me. She even offered me twenty dollars for cab fare from Harlem to Bed-Stuy. You know Mister Macho ran far away from her.

This is the Brooklyn I know. And in 1989, I still don't understand it. To me, it remains a hieroglyph of millions of Black symbols and characters on a papyrus of asphalt, tar, and steel. But I'm beginning to get some help in understanding the language in the form of a cinematic translator, Spike Lee.

From his award-winning student film, *Joe's Bed-Stuy Barbershop: We Cut Heads,* to his first feature, *She's Gotta Have It,* to his newest, *Do The Right Thing,* Lee has done more to demystify the Black experience—not only in Brooklyn, but nationally and, in a psychic sense, globally, too—than any other director in recent memory.

I know barbershops on Seventh and Eighth avenues in Harlem that for years have served as tonsorial museums, numbers spots, and neighborhood town halls, just like the one Spike mythologized in *Joe's.* (Although Teapot, that foul-mouthed little kid in the movie, must have been a character indigenous to Brooklyn; had he used language like that in Ace Barbershop on 145th Street, or in Super Fly on 121st, he would have been slapped sideways and silly into next week.)

In *She's Gotta Have It,* Lee sketched a black and white—and hot all over—composite of a skeezer with scruples, Nola Darling. The film not only icono-blasted Black sexual totemism—Nola with the notches on her bra strap, her three suitors as the Notched Ones—but also showcased Black people as something more than exotica and erotica.

For all of Nola's vim, vigor, and hump, Lee pictures a lonely conquistadora at the end of the film. Sitting on her empty bed, framed by flickering candles and dim windows, Nola's empty expression has been the best prologue yet to the sexual terrorism of AIDS, which kicked to serious bass tempo just months later.

Troublemaker. Troublemaker. That Spike Lee is a troublemaker. That's another thing about fellas from Brooklyn. They like to start trouble. When the guys around my block in Harlem heard about the string of robberies and assaults outside of Madison Square Garden after the Jacksons' 1984 Victory Tour, they immediately said, "It's them country, knucklehead niggers from Bed-Stuy and Da 'Ville. They still snatchin' chains. They still wearin' them big Fred-Williamson-Hell-Up-in-Harlem hats. They started it, no-home-trainin'-havin' bastids. They just like to fight."

The brothers from Brooklyn indeed seem to enjoy the big beat-down. Look at Mike Tyson. Look at Mark Breland. Look at Spike Lee, for that matter. What Black person in their right mind would dare to make a film about the hush-hush caste system that exists between us, as Lee did in *School Daze?* Even stage an MGM-lavish dance number called "Straight and Nappy" to underscore the point? On top of that, who would think that a flick like *School Daze* would turn out to be the aesthetic and financial success that it has become?

I guess the point is this: Spike Lee is a typical Brooklyn knucklehead who likes to throw down because he's good at it. With *Do The Right Thing,* Lee launches a hard and swift punch to the multi-headed beast of racism, connecting with a comic, but brutal, blow.

The characters in the Bed-Stuy neighborhood where the film is set are ubiquitous, inner-city archetypes. Da Mayor is the local wino, expediter, and fountainhead of wisdom drawn from a cracked cistern of hard knocks. Mother Sister sits in her window, watching and listening to everything and everyone. The streetcorner triumvirate of ML, Sweet Dick Willie, and Coconut Sid are anachronistic Men from Athens, sitting on a cinderblocked Mars Hill, talking more doo-doo than Ex-Lax, and believing every word of it.

Radio Raheem and Buggin' Out are the neighborhood knuckleheads-cum-rabble-rousers, powered by the hip hop Magna Carta of Public Enemy's Fight the Power. There is Mookie, the hardworking but responsibility-duckin' kid who delivers pizzas for Sal, the modern version of the benevolent plantation owner. And that's where the crisis of the movie takes place—in Sal's Famous Pizzeria, on the hottest day of the summer, when pigmentation, pride, and culture have the most volatile chemistry.

Taking notes from the Howard Beach incident, the Michael Stewart and Eleanor Bumpers murders, and the Tawana Brawley mystery, Lee has put together a cinematic memo meant to put the powers that be on notice: We will not sit back and patiently take the abuse any longer.

This film is meant to foster heated discussion of the race problem, not only in Brooklyn, or New York City, but in America. Some people might charge that it's out to instigate a few racial confrontations. What *Do The Right Thing* will not do is leave you apathetic.

Did the movie have any effect on me? Let's put it like this: I hadn't eaten a burger in two months, but after viewing *Do The Right Thing,* I stumbled into McDonald's and gorged myself on two Big Macs. I didn't know where I was, or, for a while, *who* I was. I came out of the movie asking myself, "Is the world that mean and mixed-up? And if it is, will we let it go from bad to worse?" But don't take my word for it. Go to an air-conditioned theater this steamy summer and sweat it out yourself.

Barry Michael Cooper

INTRODUCTION

Last fall I went to the world premiere of *Tougher Than Leather,* the Run-D.M.C. film. It was a disappointment. I went wanting to like the film, but, I must admit, expecting the worst. I say expecting the worst because Russell Simmons, president of Def Jam Recordings and Run-D.M.C.'s manager, had given me the script a while back and asked me to direct it. I read it and politely declined. The script was a reworking of the Blaxploitation genre, and tell you the truth, I never went to those films, never liked them. Run, D, and Jam Master Jay spend the entire film running around and shooting people. I certainly didn't want to be responsible for any more Black youth killing each other.

The real failure of the project, in my eyes, is that the Black producers chose record producer Rick Rubin, a white man with no film experience, to cowrite and direct. There are too many talented young Black filmmakers out here who need a break to justify handing the project over to a person, of any race, who doesn't have the necessary experience.

Not just anyone can make a good film. Film is not to be played with. It may be our most powerful medium and should be treated as such. Now, wait a minute, hold up, wait a minute. I'm not suggesting that I'm the only person in the world qualified to make a film. If it were up to me, there would be a hundred Robert Townsends and Spike Lees cranking out films. In fact, the continuity of Black cinema is only assured if it is bigger than the two or three individuals who are getting play now, which brings me to my next point.

As a few of us have made our way in the cutthroat film industry, something disturbing has happened. I see factions emerging, the Eddie Murphy camp, the Robert Townsend camp, the Keenen Wayans camp, and the Spike Lee camp. I've had actors and production people come to me and say they were turned down for a job because they were considered to be down with me, with the Spike Lee camp.

There is no need to point fingers or name names, but this kind of backward thinking is gonna hurt us all in the long run. Now more than ever we have to join forces. That's not to say we have to make the same films and agree on everything. Not at all. Each of us has a distinct voice, our own stories to tell.

Early this year Robert Townsend and I were on a panel organized by the Black Media Entertainment Association out in Los Angeles. The discussion got around to Bill Cosby and the "flop" *Leonard Part 6*. We discussed whether or not Cosby was responsible for how the film turned out. Robert and I had a big disagreement before an audience of five hundred. I felt it was a healthy argument, aired for everybody to hear and make up their own minds. Evidently, people misconstrued this as a rift between us. Not true.

When *Hollywood Shuffle* was released, I must have been asked a million times by folks just trying to start some S-H-I-T for my opinion on the film. I liked the film and have even used Robert's line "Doin' the nasty" in *School Daze* and *Do The Right Thing*. I was happy that another brother had cracked the feature film nut. There should be and will be many more Black directors—male and female —besides us.

Since *Hollywood Shuffle* and *She's Gotta Have It,* we have Tony Brown's *White Girl* and Keenen Wayans's *I'm Gonna Git You Sucka* and, in production, Julie Dash's *Daughters of the Dust,* James Bond III's *Temptation,* and Melvin Van Peeble's *Identity Crisis.* Let's not forget *Coming to America,* which I think was a serious move by Eddie Murphy to do a film by and about Black people.

Black audiences are starving for films by and about us. Every day one of our films should be in the marketplace. God forbid if Eddie Murphy stops selling tickets. Would this mean no more Black films would see the light of day? Hell no, we can't let that happen. There has to be a succession. We can't let this activity stop.

Those of us who are producing now can't be threatened by new Black talent. We should embrace it. No matter how bad you are— whether you're an athlete, musician, writer, or actor—sooner or later, a new jack is gonna pop up out of nowhere and be a badder motherfucker. That's all there is to it. It's a law of nature.

I know for a fact that there are some Black film students out there studying my shit. In the next couple of years they'll scrape together a few pennies, bust out with their own joint, and smoke *Hollywood Shuffle* and *She's Gotta Have It* combined. I don't see it as a threat. I welcome it for the sake of Black cinema.

The following is a record of what had to be done to get the third feature film I have produced in four years into the can. You will see how a script is developed, how deals are made, how production problems are surmounted. I hope to further demystify the filmmaking process. Film is no hocus-pocus magic stuff. That's what Hollywood wants you to believe so you don't attempt to tell your own stories.

Do The Right Thing is my most political film to date; at the same time I think it's my most humorous. Each time out I have tried to make the best movie possible. But with film, it's always a roll of the dice. Please God, no snake eyes for *Do The Right Thing*.

Spike Lee
Brooklyn, New York

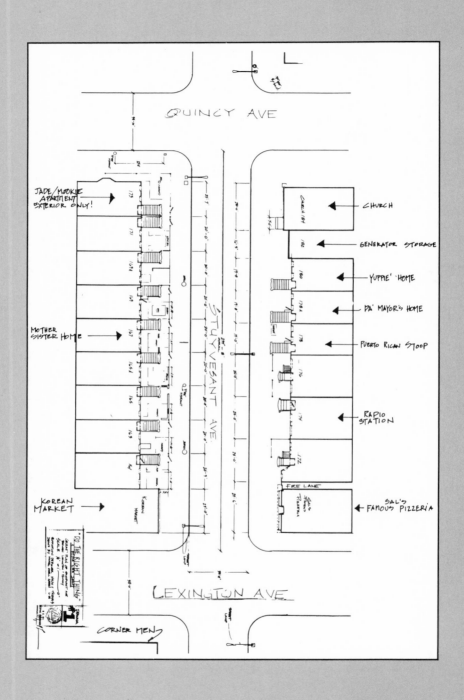

QUINCY AVE

JADE/MOOKIE
APARTMENT
EXTERIOR ONLY!

CHURCH

GENERATOR STORAGE

YUPPIE' HOME

DA' MAYOR'S HOME

PUERTO RICAN STOOP

MOTHER
SISTER HOME

STUYVESANT AVE

RADIO
STATION

KOREAN
MARKET

FIRE LANE

SAL'S
FAMOUS PIZZERIA

"DO THE RIGHT THING"

LEXINGTON AVE

CORNER MEN

PART I.

THE

JOURNAL

It's nine in the morning and I'm sitting down to get started on my next project, *Do The Right Thing*. I hope to start shooting next August. I want the film to take place over the course of one day, the hottest day of the year, in Brooklyn, New York. The film has to look hot, too. The audience should feel like it's suffocating, like *In the Heat of the Night*.

I'll have to kick butt to pull things together by August. If I'm not happy with the script, I'll hold off until the following summer. It's better to go at it right away, though, like Oliver Stone did by following *Platoon* with *Wall Street*.

I want most of the film to take place on one block. So, I need to scout a block in Brooklyn with vicious brownstones. We can build sets for the interiors, but most scenes will take place in the street and on stoops and fire escapes.

It's been my observation that when the temperature rises beyond a certain point, people lose it. Little incidents can spark major conflicts. Bump into someone on the street and you're liable to get shot. A petty argument between husband and wife can launch a divorce proceeding. The heat makes everything explosive, including the racial climate of the city. Racial tensions in the city are high as it is, but when the weather is hot, forget about it. This might be the core of a vicious climax for the film.

This block is in a Black neighborhood in Brooklyn. On one corner is a pizza parlor run by an Italian family who have refused to leave the neighborhood. One of the young Black characters will have a job at the pizzeria.

Although the Black and Puerto Rican block residents seem to get along with the Italian family, there is still an undercurrent of hostility. Of course this tension explodes in the finale. There should be a full-scale riot—all hell should break loose. Something provocative must set it off, like a cop shoots a kid and brothers go off. Then the rains come. I know, I know, sounds corny. But goddamn, this is only the first page.

I'm making an allusion to the Howard Beach incident by using a pizza parlor. The white kids in this case could be the sons of the owner of the pizzeria. Danny Aiello would be good for the role of the owner. But depending on how big the role is, I could ask Bob De Niro. He'd do it if he likes the script. One of the sons could be Richard Edson from *Stranger Than Paradise.*

The pizza parlor will have red, white, and green signs all over it like "Italian Americans #1"—the kind of banners you see at the Feast of San Gennaro in Little Italy.

Throughout the film we hear a DJ's voice over the radio, broadcasting from some fictional station. This device has been used to death, but we might be able to rework it.

The station's call name is WE LOVE RADIO. It broadcasts from a storefront on the block. The DJ looks directly out onto the street and observes all the comings and goings. Passersby can watch him as he rocks the mike. This is gonna be very stylized.

The DJ's name is Mister Señor Love Daddy, the world's only 7-24-365 DJ. That's 7 days a week, 24 hours a day, 365 days a year. He never goes to sleep. "I work overtime for your love," he says.

Playing on the final words of *School Daze,* "Please wake up," the first words of *Do The Right Thing* could be the DJ's: "Hello Nueva York. It's time to wake up. It's gonna be hot as a motherfucker." Vicious. Maybe this is where we could bring in Ossie Davis, our storyteller. Periodically he could come on camera and narrate.

OSSIE

That's right. Hot as a motherfucker. Of course
y'can't use that kind of language on the radio,
but if you could, that's what Mister Señor Love
Daddy would say. It was so hot . . .

Then we cut to various things and characters he's describing.

OSSIE

. . . I mean hot. Hot as two dogs in heat. Okay,
okay, y'get the picture.

I'm not sure about this running narration by a storyteller. Even if I don't do it, Ruby Dee and Ossie Davis are still gonna be down.

Something is happening. It's not of my will, but something is happening. I'm being singled out for my acting as much as for my writing and directing. It started with *She's Gotta Have It*. I never expected such a response to Mars Blackmon.

I had a chance to forecast on my appeal as an actor at the five recruited screenings we've had to date for *School Daze*. The minute I appear on screen, the audience got excited. Every recruited audience gave my character, Half-Pint, the highest rating. I'm not trying to say I did the strongest acting in the film, but folks identified with me. I have something with people, and I think at this stage it would be a mistake not to take this into consideration as I write *Do The Right Thing*.

I do realize my limits as an actor. I could never carry an entire movie, nor would I want to. But I know the things I can do. In this film I might want to play a crazy, crazy kid, a psychopath, a madman. But he's funny. The kind who would kill somebody for stepping on his new sneakers—Air Jordans, no doubt.

I see a Black couple as being important characters in the film. The woman will be pregnant. This will make for some good dialogue since pregnant women are naturally cranky and the summertime is the worst time in the world to be pregnant.

WOMAN

I wish I wasn't pregnant, goddamnit. This is the last one.

HUSBAND

Honey, relax you're just irritable now.

WOMAN

Irritable, my ass, I'm miserable. It's hot as
shit.

As usual I gotta have a vicious sex scene. For this one it's gonna be a naked female body with ice cubes. We should shoot it similar to the scenes in *She's Gotta Have It,* with extreme closeups. You'll see these clear ice cubes melting fast on a beautiful Black body. Smoke would be even better—smoke emitting from the body. This female is literally on fire. The guy wants to love her, but she says it's too hot and sticky. "I don't want to be bothered. It's too hot for you to be humping on me." The guy, not to be outdone, goes to the refrigerator and pulls out an ice tray. FREAKY DEAKY.

Certain characters in this joint will have nicknames of jazz musicians and athletes.

NICKNAMES

ML	JADE	TRUE MATHEMATICS
CANNONBALL	E-MAN	MOE
COUNT	LOVE DADDY	DEEK
DUKE	KID	MO-FREEK
SASSY SARAH	MONEY	SWETO
DIVINE DINAH	BLACK	CEE
TAIN	LIGHTSKIN	C
J-MASTER	VEETS	MAGIC
STEEP	PUNCHIE	ENOS
PUDDIN' HEAD	RED	WEST INDIAN WILLIE
LOCKJAW	FLATBUSH PHIL	COCONUT SID
READY FREDDY	BLACK JESUS	BLEEK
DIZZY	ELLA	BROTHER
MOOKIE	MONK	INDESTRUCTIBLE
SALLY BOY	THEOLOPILUS	FOUR EYES
SWEET FEET	AHMAD	MILK MAN
BUSHWHACK	PEACE GOD	SWEET DICK WILLIE
NIGHTTRANE	BORN KNOWLEDGE	JOE RADIO
TOO TALL	GOODERS	CORN BREAD
SHORTY	FILA	JAMBONE
TWINKIE	SATCHEL	MACHO
SMILEY	SATCHMO	COOL PAPA BELL
RE-RE	BIG BETHEL	JOSH
CLEAN HEAD	KNOCK KNOCK	BE SO MIGHTY

I have to include a fire hydrant scene in the film. Someone opens a johnny pump (in closeup). The water gushes out, then they put a can over the stream of water, making the water spray clear across the street. Kids are thrown into the water. Motorists drive by without closing their windows and their cars get drenched.

A man drives down the street in a convertible. He pleads with the kids not to wet him and they promise not to; one kid even stands in front of the hydrant. The kid moves and the convertible is instantly soaked. The driver gets out and chases after the kid, only to be hit by a blast of water from the hydrant. We hear a siren. The cops show up and listen to the driver's complaint. The driver wants an arrest made. The people in the neighborhood stand around watching, but no one points a finger to the kid who did it. The cops turn the hydrant off and promise to bust some heads if they're called again. When the kids grumble about the heat, the cops tell them to watch out or they'll be telling it to the judge.

We see the two cops in this scene throughout the film. They are corrupt, probably crack dealers themselves.

The neighborhood will have a feel of the different cultures that make up the city, specifically Black American, Puerto Rican, West Indian, Korean, and Italian American. Unlike Woody Allen's portraits of New York.

There ought to be an old lady who sits in her window, minding the block's business. She never leaves the window, or so it seems. And she doesn't miss a thing, either. Ruby Dee would be a great choice for this role.

Fellini's *Roma* is a good model for this film. I remember seeing it years ago. It's a day in the life of Rome. In *Do The Right Thing,* it's the hottest day of summer in Brooklyn, New York.

Everybody is outside on hot summer nights. No one stays in their apartments. Much of the action and dialogue should take place on the stoops. The stoops should play a very important role in this film. Of course, it would be a crime if we left out rooftops. Roofs are great locations.

We should see kids running in the streets. Kids on dirt bikes, skateboards, jumping double dutch, and playing pattycake. When I was a kid and the johnny pump was open we would use ice cream sticks as boats and race them along the gutter. There should be a feeling that the people on this block have lived as neighbors for a long time.

The block where the bulk of the film takes place should be a character in its own right. I need to remember my early years for this. We gotta have a Mr. Softee Ice Cream truck playing its theme song. When I was a kid, I ran after an ice cream truck and was almost hit by a speeding car. A neighbor ran into the street and snatched me from in front of the car in the nick of time. I ran home as fast as I could, crying up a storm. That might be an episode, who knows?

The look of the film should be bright. The light in daytime should be an intense white light, almost blinding, and the colors, bright. I mean Puerto Rican bright. AFROCENTRIC bright. Everybody will be wearing shorts and cutoff jeans. Men will be shirtless, women in tube tops.

The image of this pizzeria keeps coming into my mind. It's gonna be important in the end. It's gonna be important. I see my character working there. He hates it there, but he's gotta have a job.

Sometime soon the characters will start talking to me very specifically. I will hear their individual voices and put their words down on paper.

With the release of School Daze, there will be another slew of actors that I've worked with before who will want roles in this new film. That's fine, but I want to keep Do The Right Thing fresh with new faces. It's always exciting to see a new face give a good performance.

Not everyone who worked on School Daze is gonna be down on this one. Some actors truly showed their ass. I have to watch that I don't get too friendly with actors. Some take our friendship as a guarantee of a job for them.

The acting in School Daze is great. I will definitely use Bill Nunn, Kadeem Hardison, Branford Marsalis, Eric Payne, Giancarlo Esposito, Larry Fishburne, Leonard Thomas, Sam Jackson, and Tisha Campbell (provided her mother isn't her manager anymore). These people are a joy to work with.

Bill Nunn would be perfect as Mister Señor Love Daddy. At this stage, I shouldn't get caught up in who's playing who. It will all come soon enough. Robi Reed will be the casting director for this picture.

I would like to use some cast members from Sarafina! in this film.

I'll make a point of inviting the entire cast to the premiere of *School Daze*.

Whenever I'm in L.A. I go to see Robin Harris at the Comedy Act Theatre. He's the MC there and he's funny as shit. Don't let Robin see somebody who looks funny or is wearing some ill-fitting, ill-colored clothes, he goes off on them. The guy has me in stitches. I have to suggest to Robi that we find a role for him. He's talented and deserves a shot.

I don't know if I want to cast in L.A. this time. The best actors, for me, are in Nueva York. There is a difference in attitude. Most L.A. actors are on a Hollywood trip. They're into being stars and that's it. The actors from New York are more about work, which is the way it should be. Later for the star types. Give me actors like Bill Nunn and Sam Jackson anytime.

I would like my main man, Monty Ross, vice-president of production at Forty Acres, to play a small role in this film. He's concentrating on producing now but he's still a good actor. At most it would be a day's work. He can play someone from the South. Who, I don't know yet.

I definitely want Raye Dowell to have a substantial role in *Do The Right Thing*. I still feel bad I had to cut her part in *School Daze*. But the entire scene had to go. She's a good actress and she gets better all the time.

I've agreed to write another short film for *Saturday Night Live*. It's gonna be a parody commercial featuring Slick Mahoney selling blue and green contact lenses to Black people and introducing a new color, sapphire. It'll take one day to shoot. We can do it in the office in Brooklyn with a skeleton crew.

I'm trying to make the best film I can. I know there will be a million comparisons made between this film and *School Daze,* but I can't let that worry me. *Do The Right Thing* isn't as big in scope as *School Daze*. And hopefully it won't have as many characters. I do want it to be humorous. The story won't be as linear as *School Daze*. I would like to stop, tell a story within a story, and move on.

In this script I want to show the Black working class. Contrary to popular belief, we work. No welfare rolls here, pal, just hardworking people trying to make a decent living. Earlier I wanted to get into the whole gentrification issue, but I'm less enthusiastic about it now.

For the entire month of January I'm gonna put my ideas down on legal pads. I think I'll have enough material to start writing the actual script on or around the first of February. Now mind you, February is also the month *School Daze* opens. But I'll try to be disciplined and not miss a day.

God willing, I'll finish my first draft around the beginning of March. That would give me five months before the first of August, when I want to start shooting. I can shoot all my exterior scenes in August and save my interiors for cover sets. That would be ideal. I would like the luxury of a ten-week shoot—at least.

I'm definitely not going back to Columbia Pictures with this project. It was ideal under David Puttnam and David Picker, but with Dawn Steel (Steely Dawn), forget about it. We both went at it from the start. I don't like her tastes, don't like her movies.

Two of my first choices are Paramount Pictures and Touchstone. Jeffrey Katzenberg at Touchstone is persistently pursuing my next film. I met with the big cheeses at Paramount, Ned Tannen, Sid Ganis, and Gary Luchiesi, the last time I was out in L.A. Paramount told me that they are interested. And since Paramount Communications Inc. owns the Knicks, I might finally get the season tickets to games I need and deserve. Regardless, I'm looking for a place, a home, where I can make the films I want to make without outside or inside interference.

I must reserve the right to approve final cut of this film in my contract. *School Daze* was such a learning experience for me. Monty, who coproduced the film, and I weren't aware of the many details—especially relating to contracts—that must be seen to when you make a film on the scale of *School Daze*. That's why we hired an executive producer to hold our hands. Getting our executive producer to share this knowledge was like pulling teeth. Monty and I found out what we needed to know in the end. But on the next project we will be better prepared for all matters relating to producing the film.

After *Do The Right Thing,* I might do *The Autobiography of Malcolm X.* The project is at Warner Brothers and Denzel Washington, who played Malcolm in an off-Broadway play, is interested in the film role. We both agree that our involvement is contingent on absolute artistic control. If you think I'm gonna let some white people determine the outcome of a project like the Malcolm X piece with my name attached, you're crazy. If that film is not done truthfully and righteously, Black folks are gonna want to hang the guy behind it. Hell no. I'm not having no *Color Purple* fiasco on my conscience.

D I A L O G U E

We were so poor, we ate the hole out of a doughnut.

I D E A

When we see people drinking beer, they'll be sipping it through straws, ghetto style.

DECEMBER 27, 1987

I would like this script to be circular. Every character should have a function. If a character is introduced, he or she should appear again and advance the script in some way.

I may use an image that reappears throughout the film. In *The Last Emperor* it was the cricket. Seeing the cricket at the end of the film made it magical for me.

After the climax of the film, I would like to have a coda. This scene could take place the morning after the riot. We see the aftermath from the night before. It's not so hot on this day, and folks seem to have regained their senses. I'll have to think of a way to convey this.

It's early, but I don't want anyone to die in the riot. Some people will get hurt. Some will definitely get fucked up, but as of now, no one will be killed.

While I was in the grocery today I heard a radio newscast that two Black youths had been beaten up by a gang of white youths in Bensonhurst. The two Black kids were hospitalized. They were collecting bottles and cans when they got jumped. This happened on Christmas night. Just the other day some Black kids fired up a white cab driver in Harlem. New York City is tense with racial hatred. Can you imagine if these incidents had taken place in the summer, on the hottest day of the year? I'd be a fool not to work the subject of racism into *Do The Right Thing*.

The way I see it, we'll introduce the subject very lightly. People will expect another humorous film from Spike Lee, but I'll catch them off guard. Then I'll drop the bomb on them, they won't be prepared for it.

If a riot is the climax of the film, what will cause the riot? Take your pick: an unarmed Black child shot, the cops say he was reaching for a gun; a grandmother shot to death by cops with a shotgun; a young woman, charged with nothing but a parking violation, dies in police custody; a male chased by a white mob onto a freeway is hit by a car.

It's funny how the script is evolving into a film about race relations. This is America's biggest problem, always has been (since we got off the boat), always will be. I've touched upon it in my earlier works, but I haven't yet dealt with it head on as a primary subject.

I need to use my juice to get the testimony of Cedric Sandiford and other key witnesses in the Howard Beach case. We're not only talking Howard Beach: It's Eleanor Bumpers, Michael Stewart, Yvonne Smallwood, etc.

If I go ahead in this vein, it might be in conflict with the way I want to tell the story. It can't be just a diatribe, WHITE MAN THIS, WHITE MAN THAT. The treatment of racism will have to be carried in the subtext until the end of the film. Then again, being too avant-garde, too indirect, might trivialize the subject matter. Any approach I take must be done carefully and realistically. I won't be making any apologies. Truth and righteousness is on our side. Black folks are tired of being killed.

This is a hot one. The studios might not want to touch this film. I know I'll come up against some static from the white press. They'll say I'm trying to incite a race riot.

The entire story is starting to happen in my mind. "The hottest day of the summer" is a good starting point, but I need more. I'll be examining racial tensions and how the hot weather only makes them worse. These tensions mount, then something happens outside or inside of the pizza parlor that triggers a major incident.

Now I'm grounded. I know what I'm doing. It will be told from a Black point of view. I've been blessed with the opportunity to express the views of Black people who otherwise don't have access to power and the media. I have to take advantage of this while I'm still bankable.

The character I play in *Do The Right Thing* is from the Malcolm X school of thought: "An eye for an eye." Fuck the turn-the-other-cheek shit. If we keep up that madness we'll be dead. YO, IT'S AN EYE FOR AN EYE.

It's my character who sees a great injustice take place and starts the riot. He turns a garbage can upside down, emptying the trash in the street. Then he goes up to the pizza parlor screaming, "An eye for an eye, Howard Beach," and hurls the garbage can. It flies through the air in slow motion, shattering the pizza parlor's glass windows. All hell breaks loose. Everyone takes part in the riot, even the old woman who sits in her window watching the block. This is random violence. But before this, the cops do something that escalates the conflict to violence. They might even kill someone. The riot takes off, and it's the Italians in the pizza parlor who have to pay.

In the riot scene, it might be vicious if no words were spoken until my character throws the garbage can in the window and screams "Howard Beach."

The subject matter is so volatile, it must be on the QT. No way are people gonna read the script, especially agents. I'm not giving out information on the film until it's about to be released. Mum's da word.

My sister Joie will be the female lead in this film. With each film she's gotten bigger and better roles. Joie has been studying acting with Alice Spivak, who taught me while I was at NYU. Joie has a natural thing with a camera. Either you have it or you don't, and Joie does. Now it's up to me to write the right role for her. She'll definitely be a star in this one. Joie will play my character's sister. We live together in an apartment on the block. For the most part, I'm shiftless and lazy and have no ambition. My sister always pushes me to do better, to expect more from myself. She works and goes to school at night.

One of the sons of the pizza parlor owner has an eye for her. I know this and I tell him "no haps." After the pizza parlor is burnt to the ground in the riot, Sal's sons want the big payback. They happen to run into my sister on her way from night school. What they do to her, I don't know yet.

DIALOGUE

Those who tell don't know.
Those who know won't tell.

DECEMBER 28, 1987

Of course we must have one of those Uncle Tom Handkerchief Niggers on the block. He's one of those people who love the white man more than he loves himself. He tries to stop the riot. He's in front of the pizzeria urging folks not to tear it down. The folks pull him to the side and give him a few good licks upside the head.

There might be a fruit and vegetable stand on the block, owned by a Korean family. During the riot scene, the entire family is outside the store pleading ME BLACK, ME BLACK, ME NO WHITE, ME BLACK TOO. The folks are more amused than anything else. They leave the store untouched.

The Italian family that owns and runs the pizzeria does not live in the neighborhood. They might live in Canarsie or Bensonhurst.

There's static between my character and the sons of the pizzeria owner. We go at it all the time, exchanging insults. "You jungle-bunny—nigger motherfucker!" "You dago—wop—spaghetti bender—fake Don Corleone asshole!" Their father has to break it up and threatens to fire all of us.

When the sons are alone with the father, they want to know why he hired me. They ask him if he's a nigger lover. The father tells them that having my character around makes for good business. "This is a Black neighborhood, we're a minority. Look, I've never had no trouble with Blacks, don't want none either. So don't you start. Isn't it hot enough already without you starting up? Listen to your old man. Relax or I'm gonna kick your I'm-a-man-know-it-all ass. Now all of youse, go and work. Let your old man take a breather."

When the pizzeria is being burnt to the ground, the owner asks one of the old people, maybe Ruby Dee's character, why his store was hit. The woman answers: "You were there. The first white folks they saw. You was there. That's all."

Somewhere in the script there should be a dialogue about how the Black man in America owns very little. The character points to the Korean fruit and vegetable stand across the street:

MAN #1

Look at those Korean motherfuckers across the street. I betcha they hadn't been a month off the boat before they opened up their place. A motherfucking month off the boat and they're in business in our neighborhood, occupying a storefront that had been boarded up for longer than I care to remember, and I've been here a long time. Now for the life of me, I haven't been able to figger this out. Either dem Koreans are geniuses or we Blacks are dumb.

MAN #2

But wait a minute, it's not just the Koreans. Don't pick on them. Everyone else has a business and supports their own but us. I'll be one happy fellow to see us have our own businesses. I'd be the first in line to spend my hard-earned money. Yep, that's right. I'd be the first in line.

Somebody in his audience says: "Aw shut up nigger and sit down."

I can't have too many of these speeches. This is cinema, not the stage.

My goal as a filmmaker is to get better with each outing. I have to pinpoint the areas I need to work on. What are my weaknesses? The first thing that comes to mind is better communication with actors. I need to give them a clearer idea of my vision, my understanding of the script, and of the characters. I might have a picture in my head, but I have to take it further than that. I would also like to enhance my visual sense. In the past I've leaned too heavily on my cinematographer Ernest Dickerson, who I've worked with since film school. But I'm gonna assert myself more in that area.

I want the camera moving all the time, more than it did in *School Daze*. I see a shot where the camera tracks down a row of stoops filled with people. On each stoop there's a different conversation happening. The camera moves slowly from stoop to stoop. Vicious. Also, I want to use long choreographed shots for most of this film. I do not want a lot of cutting.

It might be possible to use a sky-cam given that we'll be shooting on one block. Since a sky-cam camera is controlled by remote, it could float effortlessly from rooftops down to the sidewalk and vice versa.

We definitely have to use a sky-cam on the shot where I scream "Howard Beach" and throw the garbage can. The sky cam has to descend from the heavens into a closeup of me screaming "Howard Beach." Vicious.

It's of utmost importance that this film be shot in summer. The earliest we could do it is August. We're talking the dog days of summer. There would be no need to fake the heat. This means I've got work ahead of me. But if it's film work, that's okay.

I want to have fun writing this script. I never want it to be a chore or a burden. It doesn't have to be. Any day shit isn't flowing, I'll just stop and continue the next day. Whenever I force myself to write, I don't produce anything worthwhile anyway.

Wouldn't it be interesting if I brought a character or two back from *She's Gotta Have It* or *School Daze*? I think I'm gonna do it. Reprising Mars Blackmon would be a big mistake. Should Tracy Camilia Johns come back as Nola Darling? Nah, bad idea. Maybe shouldn't bring anyone back.

DIALOGUE

They're gonna pay. I'm not saying that hateful, I'm saying it like the sky is blue.

DECEMBER 29, 1987

It's 4:00 P.M. and I just finished *The Autobiography of Malcolm X*. It's a great story. It would be a monster if Denzel Washington and I could have control over the project. I like David Mamet's script, but I would have to write my own. Another screen adaptation of the autobiography I got a hold of read like a TV movie. I am of the opinion that only a Black man should write and direct *The Autobiography of Malcolm X*. Bottom line.

Giancarlo Esposito is half Black and half Italian. He could play a character called Spaghetti Chitlins (I don't know about the name, it's the first thing that came into my mind). He's more readily accepted by Blacks than Italians.

I'm gonna have this Black-Italian thing down to a T. Some Italians may say it's biased, but look at how the Black characters were portrayed in Rocky films.

DECEMBER 30, 1987

Barry Brown and I have to start cutting the video for *Da Butt* and do a million things to complete *School Daze*. I've also gotta write and shoot my short film for *Saturday Night Live* very soon. There's always work to do.

As with *School Daze,* the way things are coming together with *Do The Right Thing,* there will be no starring roles. I like ensemble pieces, I really do.

My father will compose the score for the film. We have our problems, but they are always overcome. He's a great composer, that's the bottom line. His music only makes my films that much better.

The score should not have a big sound. I don't want to commit to this at such an early stage of development, but maybe a sextet would work. When needed, we could come in with a string section.
DRUMS—SMITTY SMITH
PIANO—KENNY KIRKLAND
BASS—BILL LEE
TRUMPET—WYNTON MARSALIS
TENOR—BRANFORD MARSALIS

JANUARY 1, 1988

There will be a scene where a b-boy is walking, no, bopping, down the street when a yuppie accidently steps on his new sneakers. There is a big black smudge on his unlaced, white Air Jordans. The white man says excuse me, thinking that's it, and walks. The brother runs after him and pulls him around.

BLACK

Excuse, excuse. That's it. You steppin' on my new white Jordans that I just bought and all you can say is excuse me. I'll fuck you up quick two times. Who told you to step on my sneakers? Who told you to walk on my side of the block? Who told you to be in my neighborhood?

YUPPIE

I own a brownstone on this block.

BLACK

Who told you to buy a brownstone on my block, in my neighborhood? Can't walk without tripping over you yuppies. What do you want to live in a Black neighborhood for?

YUPPIE

I'm under the assumption that this is America and one can go where he pleases.

BLACK

This is America? I should fuck you up just for that stupid-ass shit.

BLACK looks down at his sneakers. By now a crowd has formed and is egging BLACK on.

BLACK

You lucky the Black man has a loving heart. Next
time you see me coming, cross the street quick.
Damn, my brand new Jordans. You should buy me
another pair. Yeah, if I wasn't a righteous
Black man, you'd be in serious trouble. SERIOUS.

Someone in the crowd says, "Word, go back to where you came
from." Black gets a piece of chalk and draws a circle around the
yuppie.

BLACK

If you leave this circle before an hour, that's
it.

The more I think about Robert De Niro playing the father, the
owner of the pizzeria, the more I like it. The trick is to have him
function as a key character even though he plays a minimum number of scenes. Brian DePalma was able to do this with De Niro in
The Untouchables.

A little later in the day I'm gonna call De Niro. We met a year
ago, the night after the Howard Beach incident. We discussed racism and how the animosity between Blacks and Italians has esca-
lated. I think we can make an important film about the subject.
Truth is more important than an evenhanded treatment of the subject. No matter what, the story has to be told from a Black perspective. On the other hand, I don't want this to be preachy. I hate those
kinds of films.

It has to be a small incident that leads to the film's final confrontation. This incident will appear to be nothing at first, then it turns
into something bigger, then it turns into something bigger again.
Add the combustible atmosphere of the hottest day of the year and
you have a big disturbance, a race riot.

I know my character will throw the garbage can through the
pizzeria window. This is prompted by a beating by the cops. But
what prompted the cops? An idea came to me this morning. At
Brooklyn College a couple of years ago there was a major disturbance between Black and white students that involved a jukebox.

The Jewish kids wanted to listen to their music, the Blacks wanted to hear theirs. Somehow a fight started. That's the little incident I need.

What would happen if a Black youth came into the pizzeria with a giant box blasting rap? A box so loud people can't hear themselves think. This guy could be Joe Radio! The music has to be some vicious rap record. How 'bout a dope beat with a rap using the names of Black people along with a chorus of "Uplift the Race, By Any Means Necessary"?

Joe Radio comes into the pizzeria with his box booming. The owner tells him to turn it off. Joe Radio, or even better, Radio Raheem, just turns it up louder and orders his slice. The owner refuses to wait on anybody till Raheem takes the noise outta his store.

The owner's sons play Rocky Balboa and use force to remove Raheem. The climax is set in motion. A scuffle breaks out, the cops are called. Any time cops see a white person struggling with a Black person, you know who they're gonna go after. They put a choke hold on Raheem. He falls to the ground like a sack of potatoes. The cops try to revive him; they play it like he's faking. Get up, get up, they're yelling at him.

Finally the cops see what they've done to Raheem. They try to get him outta there without people knowing the deal, but it's too late. Word goes through the already volatile crowd: Radio Raheem is dead, they killed him. I hear this and pick up the garbage can, dump the garbage in the street, and scream "Howard Beach." The missile flies through the air in slo-mo, breaking the plate glass storefront, and the riot begins.

So that's what I'm talking about. How a little incident compounds tensions between Blacks and Italians and becomes a full-scale race riot. And how the hot weather adds fuel to the fire.

Larry Fishburne would be the perfect Radio Raheem. We see him throughout the film, cruising the block. Of course, you hear him before you see him. He never says hello, just points his finger at you to acknowledge you.

We might even see a scene where Raheem's box is slow. He stops to pull out new batteries then he's back in action. Radio Raheem's movement should be sluggish when the batteries are dying. He perks up again with fresh Duracells. Fish might be upset that the role of Radio Raheem isn't bigger, but I hope he understands. Radio Raheem is a key figure. He should be a mysterious character. Maybe the only words we should hear him say are "Sixteen Duracells," when he goes into the store to buy some batteries for his box. He might even have a carriage for his box instead of holding that big sucker.

JANUARY 2, 1988

Yesterday Lisa Jones and I went to a party at Toni Morrison's house in upstate New York. On the way back I let Lisa read my notes so far. She likes the idea a lot. At first she said she was a little skeptical about a pizzeria in an all-Black neighborhood, but now she sees it.

There must be a resolution of some sort after the riot. For the most part, the Black uprisings in the sixties took place in poor, inner-city, neighborhoods. The buildings hit are still burnt-out shells, they were never replaced. The only people hurt in the long run were the Black people who lived in those communities. That's why this film must have a coda on the end. I'd get myself hung by showing violence for violence's sake.

In the first light of day, we can see the damage that was done the previous night. The pizzeria is totalled. Fire is still smouldering from the wreckage. My character is walking toward the pizzeria. He's not gloating or anything. He hears someone rummaging through the remains—it's the owner. Henceforth the owner's name is SAL and the pizzeria is SAL'S FAMOUS PIZZERIA.

Sal looks like he's on a mission. He finally stops when he notices my character standing there looking at him. This is where the most poignant scene should take place. It has to be subtle. It can't be any of this We-Are-the-World, We-Are-All-God's-Children, We-Can-Work-It-Out shit, either. But it has to be honest.

My character came to look for something, too. He might even ask Sal if he has seen this particular object. Sal replies, "No, but you should have thought to get it before you and your people torched my place." I ask, "You don't mind if I look for it, do you?" Sal says,

"No, be my guest. I'm surprised myself how calm I am. There was a day when I would have killed some colored!"

As my character joins Sal in the rubble, he asks him what he's looking for. Sal mumbles something. I wonder if I can pull it off that they're looking for the same thing. It's not a buried treasure or money, but something with no monetary value. They find it and sit on the curb and look up into the hot blazing sun. I say, "It's gonna be hot as a motherfucker." Sal says, "In the high nineties. But y'know what? I'm going to the beach for the first summer day in twenty-three years. I'm gonna take off and go to the beach."

Offscreen we hear a familiar rap record. The camera pulls back and we see Radio Raheem with a neck brace on. He's carrying a smaller radio. He doesn't have the same strut, but he's moving. The camera ascends to reveal the entire block as it swirls in morning activity. THE END.

The script should be structured so that the final scene between my character and Sal won't disturb audiences. I don't want to hear, "Yeah, he wrote it so he could have the final scene with De Niro." Of course this is assuming that we can get Bob to do the role. (If it does happen, I can't be intimidated by him.) Hooking up with De Niro would be a monster. It would really fuck with Italians, to see De Niro in a film sympathetic to Black people, told from a Black perspective. I know it also kills them to see Bobby with Black women, kills 'em dead.

Famous Pizzeria has pictures of famous Italian Americans all over the place. People like Joe DiMaggio, Rocky Marciano, Perry Como, Frank Sinatra, Luciano Pavarotti, Liza Minnelli, Governor Mario Cuomo, Al Pacino, Boom Boom Mancini, and Sylvester Stallone as Rocky Balboa and Rambo.

CUSTOMER

Sal, how come you ain't got no brothers up on the wall here?

SAL

You want brothers up on the wall, you open up your own business. Then you can do what you

wanna do. My pizzeria, Italian Americans on the
wall.

CUSTOMER

Take it easy, Sal. I was just jiving.

SAL

Don't start on me today. You don't like stars or
something?

CUSTOMER

They're great, Sal. They're great.

Come Monday it's back to the grind, the holiday season will be
over. Right now I need to work out my schedule. If I get up at 7 A.M.
and write from 7:30 or 8 to 10, that will give me at least two hours
a day. I always do my best writing in the morning.

I know it's early, but who could play Sal's sons? Richard Edson is
one idea. Lisa Jones made a great suggestion of Andy Garcia. He
was in *Untouchables* and resembles a young Pacino.

DIALOGUE

Could that be?
It be's, it be's.

JANUARY 3, 1988

I've got it. My character's name will be MOOKIE. People might
think of Mookie Wilson, who plays center field for the Mets. When
I lived in the Cobble Hill section of Brooklyn as a kid, there was a
guy named Mookie who was a great softball pitcher. He was left-
handed and could throw fast as shit. That's the first Mookie I knew.

Last night I went to see Eddie Murphy in *Raw*. The film was
okay, but there was one hilarious skit about Italians. Eddie had

them down; yelling MOULAN YAN [nigger] this, MOULAN YAN that. The most truthful thing he said is that Italians act like niggers more than niggers do. It's true, they certainly act Black and don't even know it.

I must be careful to avoid stereotypes in *Do The Right Thing*. You know, the Italian guy holding his nuts and yelling, Yo Carmine. Only real characters, no types. Even Radio Raheem should not be a type, even though he carries a box and everybody has seen guys like him.

Mookie and Sal's two sons fight about everything. Everything being in terms of Black and white. I guess that's what racism does. However, the entire film can't be just a round of racial epithets.

Another thing I must stay aware of: The only serious white characters in the piece are Sal and his sons. And yes, they are important characters, but the film is not fundamentally about them. It's about the Black people that live on this one block in Brooklyn, New York.

Sal is constantly having it out with his two sons. They tell him to sell the pizzeria in Bed-Stuy and open up one in their neighborhood, Bensonhurst. Sal says there are too many pizzerias there already, but the sons continue to badger him. We're sick of these niggers, they say, it's a bad neighborhood. We just don't like being around them. They're animals. They mess up the shop. They throw garbage on the floor. We're gonna get robbed. The oldest one says, "My friends laugh at me all the time, they laugh right in my face and tell me go feed the MOOKS slices. Daddy, what can I say? I don't wanna be here, they don't want us here. They don't want us here. We should stay in our own neighborhoods. Niggers stay in the ghettos. We stay in Bensonhurst."

Now, Sal can't be a saint. His two sons just didn't pick up this shit out of the thin air. They get it from home, from their parents, from their friends. This is the tricky thing. Like many people who have racist views, these views are so ingrained, they aren't aware of them. We should see that in Sal. Basically he's a good person, but he feels Black people are inferior.

Even if Sal's not a saint, in the end when he sits down with Mookie on the curb, there has to be a sliver of realization on his part. He has to recognize Mookie's humanity. I say the changes happen in Sal instead of Mookie because I feel Black people cannot be held responsible for racism. We are not in that position. We are, and have been, the victims.

Yesterday Black protestors led a march through Bensonhurst to protest recent acts of racially motivated violence. I watched it on the news. It could have Birmingham or Selma, Alabama, in the sixties the way those Italian mobs were carrying on. It was frightening.

DIALOGUE

Bensonhurst, have you heard? This is not Johannesburg.

I should work baseball bats into this somehow. The white mob in the Howard Beach case chased the Black men with baseball bats.

During an argument between Mookie and one of Sal's sons, Mookie asks, "If you hate Black people so much, why are Michael Jordan and Dwight Gooden your favorite players?"

PINO

That's different.

MOOKIE

How? Both was Black the last time I checked.

PINO

To me, they're not Black. They're the best,
they're great. I don't see them as Black.
They're different.

MOOKIE

Sounds sick to me. You go to a game, cheer for a
Black athlete. Then come home from the game and
call me every kind of nigger.

PINO

That's different. Mookie, you're a nigger.

MOOKIE

Black is Black.

I've come to a decision. No character shall reappear from *She's Gotta Have It* or *School Daze* in *Do The Right Thing*. It was a lame, half-thought-out idea. Forget it. It's forgotten.

JANUARY 4, 1988

Today is Monday. The holiday season is over, it's back to work. BLACK TO WORK.

One character's name should be BLACK. Mookie calls everybody "Black" and "Money." "Whadd'up Black?" "Whadd'up Money?" Sal's sons might be named Johnny Boy and Vito. [Note: Johnny Boy changed to Pino.]

There should be an old man people call Da Mayor who lives on the block by himself. He's the self-proclaimed mayor of the block. He's also a big cheese-eater. He was brought up in the day when a Black man had to bow and stoop to the white man just to stay in one piece. His favorite line is, "It's purely for medicinal purposes." Then he downs a bottle of brew.

To keep some change in his pocket, Da Mayor sweeps Sal's sidewalk every morning, then waits to be tipped. Sal's sons don't like it. Why pay him? they want to know, why not make MOOK THE SPOOK do it, he's getting paid for sitting on his Black ass.

Sal and his two sons don't trust Mookie. He is not allowed to use the cash register. He waits on customers, takes their money, then he has to hand it to Sal or one of the sons. He gets the change back and then gives it to the customers.

Both Pino and Vito only made it through high school. They will work in their father's pizzeria probably for the rest of their lives and are ill-equipped to do otherwise. They're lower-middle class and basically uneducated. You ought to see the way they react to Blacks in business suits. It burns them up that a nigger could have more than they will ever have in life. They can't believe it. A FUCKING MOULAN YAN.

Pino, Vito, and Mookie have many similarities. All three are high school graduates and are stuck in dead-end jobs. They are trapped. They would never discuss it amongst themselves. But Mookie will have a scene where his sister hassles him about his low-paying job. His sister has replaced their Moms and is constantly in Mookie's shit. She stays on his case and he starts to resent it.

I'm having second thoughts about having one of Sal's sons like Mookie's sister. It was done in *Mean Streets* and reminds me too much of Romeo and Juliet and all that forbidden love stuff.

Pino is Sal's oldest son. He tells Vito what to do, and Vito puts up little protest. The two are close even though Pino pushes Vito around and abuses him.

I'm sorry, Larry Bird, but your name will be mentioned in a film of mine once again. This time it's in an argument between Mookie, Pino, and Vito. I don't know what the argument will be about yet. But Larry Bird is a god to Pino and Vito. If Mookie talks bad about Bird, his words are fighting words for them.

DIALOGUE

It's E-VIT-ABLE.

Mookie has a tendency to mispronounce words. He knows the meaning, he just gets the pronunciation all wrong. Mookie wears black sunglasses all the time. Maybe in a key moment they break or he loses them. He might be hiding from something.

In the coming weeks I need to start formulating a list of all the characters in this mutha.

JANUARY 5, 1988

I can see now, Columbia Pictures is gonna make it difficult for me to write this new script. Yesterday they called to say they wanted to delay the opening of *School Daze* by two weeks because *Action Jackson,* starring Carl Weathers and Vanity, is set to open the same day. It's supposedly a *Robocop* ripoff, but it's really another bullshit Blaxploitation film. Columbia is worried because Lorimar Pictures is spending a bundle on *Action Jackson,* and they feel *School Daze* can't compete. What that says to me is that Columbia sees Black people as one monolithic audience. There is no diversity, as they see it. We all go to the same movies and we all have the same taste. Of course I went off. The film will open February 12 as planned. Columbia Pictures is fighting me every inch. Luckily I've done so much prepublicity for *School Daze,* they can't bury it. (I pray to God.) I may have to do more. Columbia's marketing program for the film is inadequate at best. The trailer still isn't complete. They just don't have the right people on the project.

Many times I get too emotional for my own good. It's good to express your emotions, but do it all the time and you're liable to kill yourself. Yesterday was a good example. I was so upset about this goddamn *Action Jackson* shit I couldn't sleep. I can't let bullshit like this affect me or I'll be a basket case. Take it nice and nice, easy does it everytime, so says Frank Sinatra.

My job is to write the best script possible and not worry about where I'll be, studiowise, for this next project.

DIALOGUE

MOOKIE

Fuck you, your pizzeria, and Frank Sinatra too.

PINO

Fuck you and fuck Jesse Jackson.

Spike, you've got to get out of the mindset that this entire film is about the Black-Italian conflict. This shouldn't be the case. Plus I've gotta keep my humor. I can't let myself get trapped.

Starting this weekend I have to buckle down and put in at least two hours a day. I'm gonna be a writing motherfucker in February. I'm talking about a 100-minute movie, this time—100 pages or less.

JANUARY 6, 1988

No doubt this film is gonna get more heat than any other film I've done. I know there will be an uproar about this one. I wouldn't be surprised if Forty Acres and a Mule received death threats. We're talking white people and racism in a major motion picture. It will be interesting to see how studios deal with it. This film must have a wide, wide release. I have to have major assurances going in.

JANUARY 8, 1988

Yesterday I talked to Ernest about the film. He's fired up. He's already thinking about how to visualize the heat. He wants to see people in the theaters sweating as they watch the film.

We should have closeups of people's faces, I mean extreme close-ups, with beads of perspiration dripping off.

Every character must comment on the heat. Those outside should look up at the sky, the sun. That would make a nice montage, everybody looking up to the sun.

What's one of the worst things about summertime? Flies, flies, flies. I hate flies. I can see a scene where somebody is going crazy trying to kill a fly. That would be good scene for Bob De Niro. He almost destroys his pizzeria trying to kill a fly. He's cursing up a storm all the while. Sonabitch, you're dead, you're gonna buy the farm.

Anytime the camera is rolling we should be thinking about the heat. I want to have sequences in *Do The Right Thing* where we suspend the narrative and show how people are coping with the oppressive heat. This should be a montage.

1. People in cold showers.

2. Sticking their faces into sinks.

3. Sticking their heads into refrigerators.

4. Standing in front of air conditioners.

5. Women refusing to cook.

6. Men downing packs of ice-cold brew.

I want to use Chinese angles like the ones that were used so effectively in *The Third Man*. They'll add an aura of uneasiness to the film. In fact, Ernest and I should screen *Third Man*, along with *In the Heat of the Night, Body Heat,* and *Apocalypse Now* as many times as possible.

The companies that distributed *She's Gotta Have It* and *School Daze* insisted on marketing the films as comedies. With Island Pictures, *She's Gotta Have It* was a "seriously sexy comedy," and with Columbia, *School Daze* was a "comedy with music." It seems to make the films more palatable and less threatening for a white audience. I don't think either film is a comedy. I'm not denying the films are funny, but I feel that I make films that don't fall into any particular genre.

The humor in *Do The Right Thing* is gonna be like the humor in *Dog Day Afternoon, Cuckoo's Nest, Network, Last Detail*. These are serious movies that are funny as shit.

There is a pizzeria on Myrtle Avenue in Brooklyn that could serve as the model for Sal's Famous Pizzeria. I went there all the time while I lived nearby on Adelphi Street. Sal's Famous Pizzeria charges $1.50 a slice and Black folks always complain when they pay their money.

FOLKS

Damn, Sal. A buck fifty, shit. Put some more cheese on that motherfucker.

SAL

Extra cheese is two dollars. You know that.

FOLKS

Two dollars. Forget it. Just gimme the regular with
extra cheese.

JANUARY 9, 1988

I might go to Atlanta for a week or so for some peace and quiet. I
have to promote *School Daze,* but at the same time I gotta get the
next motherfucker ready.

My daily routine since the holidays has been to write for one to
two hours before I go into the office. At the office, I talk on the
phone, answer questions, sign checks. I could be making better use
of my time. Maybe I should start coming in around noon—that way
I can write a good four or five hours a day instead of one. I might be
able to start writing the actual script before February 1, 1988, if I
think I'm ready. I plan to get a lot of stuff done this weekend.
Tomorrow I'm not even gonna go out. I'll just write, write, write,
and watch the Knicks.

Have you ever noticed that when white people are talking to
Black people and they don't want to say niggers, they say "youse
people"? It's always "youse people." We gotta get that into it.

The mayor of the block is all alone in the world. He has no relatives that he knows or cares about. He will talk your head off if you
let him. Da Mayor has a special thing for the young people. He feels
he's seen it all and can teach these young kids something. Very few
of the young kids bother to listen to him. They think he's just an
old drunk, but he's not. He's got some valuable knowledge, if they'd
only listen. One of the few kids who does listen is Mookie. He will
always check on Da Mayor to see how he's doing or go to the store
and get him a beer.

Da Mayor and the old woman who sits in her window don't get
along at all. Who knows, maybe they were lovers once, but now
they're always getting into arguments. This could be funny as hell.

WOMAN

Get outta here, ya old drunk.

DA MAYOR

Drunk? You're so ugly it would drive a man to drink.

A lot of this dialogue could be improvised. Why? Because it's Ruby Dee and Ossie Davis playing the roles. They been married for how many years? I couldn't even begin to write dialogue like that; they have lived it.

I like to hear the title of a film incorporated in the dialogue. In this one I want the title to be said more than once. Maybe the older people can say it to the young.

The older people on this block might appear docile. But when the riot breaks out, they're at the forefront, tearing up Sal's Famous Pizzeria.

Any time Sal gets into one of his philosophical moods, he finishes a sentence with "This is America." When Black folks are tearing apart his pizzeria, Sal says, "You can't do this. This is America."

Mookie hates working at the pizzeria, but at this point in his life, he doesn't have many options. Mookie does as little work as possible. He says he doesn't get paid enough to work hard.

MOOKIE

Slavery days are over. My name ain't Kunta Kinte.

Mookie is always sneaking away to the phone to make a call. The pizzeria can be crowded, but he'll be on the phone. Mookie calls his women friends to say provocative things. It might be nice to have extreme closeups of phone receivers and the beautiful teeth and lips of the women he's calling throughout the day.

I have to be careful that the character of Mookie is not Half-Pint or Mars Blackmon. I do not want to start repeating myself after three roles.

JANUARY 12, 1988

I didn't write yesterday because we had to finish the *Da Butt* video. Y'know, I better start writing soon, though. Ed Russell, head of publicity at Columbia, wants me out for three weeks straight promoting *School Daze*. Can't do. I refuse to live out of a suitcase for three weeks. I read recently that Richard Attenborough will be out pushing his film *Cry Freedom* for the next year. I will promote *School Daze* as much as I possibly can, but I've got to start serious work on the next one.

There should be overlapping dialogue throughout the film. People should speak at the same time, stepping on each other's lines.

We need at least a week of rehearsal, maybe more. That's one luxury I will have. This is an ensemble piece, and the actors need to get comfortable with each other and build a rapport.

I'm going to reread Ann Petry's novella *"In Darkness and Confusion."* It's about the Harlem riots of 1944, which were set off when a Black soldier was killed by cops. Harlem went off.

In the scene where six cops put the choke hold on Radio Raheem and render him unconscious, we should hear the murmurs of Black folks in the crowd:

THEY KILLED HIM	WON'T STAND FOR IT
THEY KILLED RADIO RAHEEM	THE LAST TIME
IT'S MURDER	THE LAST TIME
DID IT AGAIN	FUCKIN' COPS
JUST LIKE MICHAEL STEWART	FUCKIN' COPS
MURDER	IT'S PLAIN AS DAY
ELEANOR BUMPERS	THE FIRE THIS TIME
MURDER	THE FIRE THIS TIME
IT'S NOT SAFE	THE FIRE THIS TIME
NO MORE	THE FIRE THIS TIME

The riot scene—or here's a better term, uprising—should be sort of surreal. The uprising could possibly turn into a celebration.

I should work a street vendor into this film. An old Puerto Rican man pushing a cart with bottles of colored syrups and a huge block of ice. The side of his card reads "Helado de Coco."

When I was little, my Uncle Cliff lived with us for a time. When he wanted me to run to the store he would say, "What makes Sammy run?" Then I would say, "A nickel, a dime, a quarter." Da

Mayor could use this line on the kids of the block. He has one spot on his stop that he rarely moves from. When he wants some more *cerveza fría,* he sends a kid. After a while the kids get tired of going to the corner bodega for dimes and quarters, they want to get paid in full.

I'll be happy when I can talk to Bob De Niro. He's in Arizona shooting *Midnight Run.* He'll be back at the end of January. I'll sit down with him and explain the film, then we'll see if he'll commit. The last scene between Sal and Mookie has to be vicious. I mean vicious. The both of them sitting on the curb, trying to sort out what happened.

Mookie teases Sal and his sons by calling them the Corleone Crime Family. Sal, of course, is the Don, Pino is Sonny, and Vito is Fredo. This bugs the shit outta them. Mookie might even hum the *Godfather* theme.

Yesterday I had a two-and-a-half-hour meeting with my lawyer Arthur Klein. We began strategizing about *Do The Right Thing.* The big question is, what studio can we work with?

JANUARY 13, 1988

Ernest and I are on our way to L.A. to see the first answer print (a color-corrected print) of *School Daze* from Deluxe Labs. Hopefully I'll get a chance to talk to Columbia's publicity department about *School Daze.* I've been writing notes on the new script for about three weeks. I've gotten a lot of good material and more is coming.

We've got to get Ed Koch into this, his face on a poster or a TV commercial. He's one of the main reasons why race relations are so strained in New York City. It will be subtle, but people will get the connection.

We'll have to go into preproduction immediately after I finish the script to make our August shooting date. But even so, we will have more preproduction time than we did on *School Daze.*

It's expensive as hell to shoot in New York City. It's gonna come down to what is more cost effective: to shoot in Brooklyn or go to some place like D.C. or Baltimore. I might have to do some preliminary location scouting in Baltimore. My first choice of course is to shoot right here in Brooklyn, provided I can cut a deal with the unions and the Teamsters.

I really have to give time to the relationship between Mookie and his sister. I should come up with a name for Joie's character soon. It always helps me to see the character, to develop the character, when I have a name.

The look of this film is as important as the characters. I want to spend more time on it than I've had the opportunity to do on any of my other films. Ernest and I should meet every day while we're in preproduction, looking at films in theaters and on tape and discussing what needs to be done, so that this film makes audiences sweat. I would like to use all the great Black actors in this mutha: Morgan Freeman, Leonard Jackson, Paul Benjamin, Tiger Haynes, all the folks.

Rather than one of his sons, it should be Sal who likes Mookie's sister. Sal's interest in my sister will be that much more intriguing because he's older. Sal always asks Mookie why he doesn't bring her around. Mookie and the sons pick up on Sal's feelings for Mookie's sister right away, and they are all revolted by it. Mookie's sister thinks he is just being nice, but Mookie knows better.

Sal's family is very physical, they're always hitting each other. Sal smacks Pino, and Pino smacks Vito. Mookie watches this with amusement. Mookie and Vito get along well. Vito even looks up to Mookie and this bothers the shit out of Pino. Mookie tells Vito, "Y'know the next time Pino hits you, you should kick his ass. House 'em. If you don't, he's gonna beat ya like a rug till the both of ya are in the grave."

PINO

Who are you gonna listen to, me or dat MOOK? I'm ya brother whether you like it or not. Don't go against the family. Besides, he's Black. A Moulan Yan.

The one time Vito does fight back, Pino fucks him up. Vito says, "Listening to da Mook will get you killed."

JANUARY 14, 1988

Ernest and I arrived in Los Angeles this afternoon. Right away I had a meeting with Ed Russell, Columbia's head of publicity. It didn't go well, although it was no fault of his. The classic nightmare of a filmmaker has happened to me, I'm caught in a regime change. Dawn Steel and her crew don't give a fuck about *School Daze* or any film that was made under Puttnam. They can say what they wanna say, but I know better. Their actions prove that.

From Ed Russell I learned that there will be no television advertising period. Also no ads in *Essence, Ebony,* or *Jet,* which I feel is a disgrace, a slap in the face to the Black consumer and the Black media. This is unbelievable. Columbia wants to put me on the road —twenty-one cities in twenty-one days, which is crazy—and work me like a Georgia mule so they don't have to spend a dime to promote *School Daze.* What kind of ass backwards thinking is that? When you come down to it, it's racism, sad, but true.

All they see is niggers: nigger director and nigger audience, second-rate, second-class shit; therefore the project is not worth their time and money. I'm gonna have to carry *School Daze* myself on my back. And when it takes off, without any effort on their part, Columbia will claim they knew it all along.

JANUARY 17, 1988

Haven't written in a couple of days. I've been busy trying to save *School Daze* from being dogged. Columbia Pictures doesn't want to spend a penny more than the penny they've committed to. My lawyer Arthur Klein had to meet with Victor Kaufman, the head executive at Columbia/Tri-Star, and read him the riot act. You cannot release this film without TV spots, without subway posters, without substantial ad sizes. It's a mess, but WE GOTTA PREVAIL.

While I was in L.A. I talked to De Niro. We were supposed to hook up at Universal Studios, but he got there late and I had to leave before he arrived. I told him how Columbia Pictures is trying to dog me. He told me not to worry, even if they don't want to Do The Right Thing, people will go see the film. I couldn't believe he said the title of the film. If that's not a premonition, I don't know what is.

De Niro and I didn't get to speak at length because he was calling me between shots. But he's coming to New York soon and said he'll call. It's important that De Niro be a part of this film. I know he doesn't work for money alone, so maybe he'll consider it strongly. What I need to do is stop worrying and write the best motherfucking script I can write. That would be the best way to get Bob involved.

I'm going to cannibalize a character named Buggin' Out from *Messenger,* a film that I intended to do before *She's Gotta Have It,* but never completed. Buggin' is hyper and crazy, he's perfect for the guy who almost fucks up the white boy for stepping on his new Air Jordans. Kadeem Hardison would be good for Buggin' Out. I originally cast him in that role in *Messenger.*

Guess what the headline of the *Amsterdam News* was the other day? "IF THIS WAS THE SUMMER, THERE WOULD HAVE BEEN A RIOT." That's my whole fucking movie! I KNOW I'M DOING THE RIGHT FILM.

JANUARY 19, 1988

I had a great phone conversation yesterday with Amy Olatunji, an old friend of the family. I was writing down lines from her left and right. I want, always want, my work to have some spirituality about it. It shouldn't be overt, but it should be there nonetheless.

For the past week, I've been telling myself to read the notes on the film I've completed so far. I must admit, I've been slipping. It's gonna be a battle promoting *School Daze* and writing *Do The Right Thing* at the same time.

Radio Raheem is the epitome of cool. He has a vicious walk. By the way he's dressed you'd think it's fall. He never sweats, never exerts himself or wastes a motion. What his job is, you never know, but he's always dressed. He always has enough money to buy the twenty "C" Duracell batteries he needs for his box.

Radio Raheem treats his box like it's his car, his most prized possession. In a way it is his car, it's how he gets around. He cleans it all the time and if someone even looks at it in the wrong way, that person is in trouble.

Radio Raheem comes into the Sal's Famous with his music blasting one too many times. Sal smashes the box with a baseball bat. Sal might as well have shot Radio Raheem's mother. Radio goes crazy and jumps all over Sal. The cops arrive and put a choke hold on Raheem, à la Michael Stewart, the young graffiti artist from Brooklyn who was killed while in police custody.

Radio Raheem is the misunderstood Black youth. White people cross the street when they see him coming. The Bernie Goetzes of the world want to kill him. It's important that Radio Raheem be a sympathetic character, but he's not an angel, either. He's lost, like a lot of Black youth. Their value systems are all screwed up. They're after more gold teeth, gold chains, and gold brass knuckle rings. They don't understand how worthless that shit is in the long run. They are still BLACK, POOR, and UNEDUCATED. Gold won't change that.

The song Radio Raheem plays on his box has to be by Public Enemy, my favorite politically conscious rappers. Their new jam, "Bring the Noise," is vicious. I gotta get them to do this like Brutus.

Mookie is Sal's delivery boy, busting his ass for minimum wage. He makes deliveries on a bike. That will be a good scene: Mookie delivering pizzas to folks on the block.

JANUARY 20, 1988

In a week or so, I'll leave for a two-week promotional tour. That's all the suitcase-living I can stand. It's funny, but I will probably get a lot of work done on the road. One deterrent to my writing has been fucking around with Columbia Pictures. Yesterday, Victor Kaufman was supposed to see my lawyer Arthur Klein, but he avoided him all day. Today Arthur Klein will throw his weight around. We're sick of this hide-and-seek business. We want the money that is needed to promote this film properly.

JANUARY 23, 1988

I had an interview yesterday with Joe Gelmis from *Newsday*. Gelmis made a nice comment that he considers me one of the most important young filmmakers in the world today. He didn't ghettoize me as a Black filmmaker. I've felt this, but hey, now somebody else has seen it also.

This film is gonna make people pick sides, especially Italians and Blacks. In my eyes, there are no winners in this one. Blacks burn down the pizzeria, but so what? Radio Raheem is dead or paralyzed and the conditions that we live under have not gotten any better.

Isn't it strange? There has been a recent upsurge in racial attacks in this country. At the same time, Eddie Murphy and Bill Cosby are the biggest names in TV and film. What a paradox.

A vicious idea just came in. How 'bout a scene where two people of different ethnic groups are slinging racial slurs at each other. Then we cut to several more people of different ethnicity ranking on each other. These will be quick cuts, similar to the Dog scene in *She's Gotta Have It*.

DIALOGUE   (from my main man Scott Sellers)

You the man. No, you the man. I'm just a struggling
Black man trying to keep my dick hard.

FEBRUARY 9, 1988

I'm on a flight to San Francisco. Last night was the New York premiere of *School Daze*. It was jam-packed and the response to the film was overwhelming. The ending of the movie is a motherfucker. Many women in the audience did start to hiss when Big Brother Almighty gives Jane the switcheroo.

Mama flew up from Atlanta to attend the premiere. She enjoyed parts of the film; probably the singing and dancing, but not the cursing.

January 23 was the last time I had written any notes. I thought I would be able to write while I was on the road, but I've been doing interviews from sunup to sundown. It's been nonstop. I realize it's necessary for me to promote the movie, especially when Columbia is not spending the necessary amount of money. I have no other choice than to get out on the road and beat the drum.

I do have a following. It's kind of funny, but I do. Word of mouth on *She's Gotta Have It* spread like wildfire. Island didn't spend a ton on promoting *She's Gotta Have It* because they didn't have it. But fucking Columbia Pictures. They have a good film on their hands and they don't know what to do with it. As of last night, we still have no subway posters. Fuck it, I'll put them up myself. I still believe folks will come see this film regardless.

So *School Daze* opens this Friday, February 12, in the year of our Lord 1988, in thirty markets, and on 221 screens. I'll do some more interviews, but I don't want to travel anymore. I have to start writing this next script. The new date I'm giving myself for completion of the first draft of this script is the end of March.

This script should be and will be more experimental than *School Daze,* a lot more like *She's Gotta Have It. Do The Right Thing* has to be uncompromising all the way. No pulling punches.

Once it gets warm, I'm gonna do my own preliminary location scouting. I'll just get on my bike and ride around Brooklyn.

I haven't dealt with drugs in my films so far. It might be the time to do it in *Do The Right Thing.* Drugs are destroying Black folks. No group is immune, but it hits Blacks the hardest. We should have a woman on crack in the film. I'm going to think about this one. I might be trying to tackle too much at one time.

I talked to Bob De Niro again last week. He's committed to two films after *Midnight Run,* the one he's working on now. I've gotta get two weeks from him this summer. Maybe Danny Aiello could replace him. I don't want to think about it yet. Bob has to come through.

FEBRUARY 10, 1988

I'm in San Francisco and it's 6:23 in the morning. I just did an interview with Bryant Gumbel on the *Today* show. Bryant Gumbel jumped all over me, but I kept my composure. He disapproved of

School Daze because I aired Black folks' dirty laundry. Gumbel didn't show a clip or mention when the film was opening, which the show usually does as a matter of course. The people at Columbia Pictures are upset. I was told Bryant Gumbel tried to get my number at the hotel in San Francisco to call to apologize. I wouldn't ask for an apology, but he could at least bring Tisha Campbell on the show and mention the film's release date.

I really must beef up the women's roles in this film. Not only Joie and Ruby Dee's characters, but the others as well. This is something I have to catch myself on. The women can't be secondary characters in this film. If I remind myself of this, it will be reflected in the work.

I just thought of a good direction. Everyone in this film should speak fast, at breakneck pace. That should be the general mood of the film. Fast-moving and frantic.

FEBRUARY 14, 1988

School Daze opened Friday and for all practical purposes it's history. My mode of thinking has to be *School*—oops (that's what I'm talking about)—*Do The Right Thing*. This one has to be a motherfucker. I'm on a mission to bring our shit, undiluted, uncut, to the screen.

It's best that I wait until March to start writing the new script. I'm still promoting *School Daze*. I have to. Columbia Pictures is not pushing it the way they should.

I realized this morning that I overlooked an important matter. What day of the week should the hottest day of the year in the film fall on? It should be a Saturday. Storywise, this affords me the most opportunities.

I have to be careful to keep the size and scope of *Do The Right Thing* in check. This film takes place on one day, and on one city block. That limits its range off the bat. I don't want the film to be as expansive or have as many speaking parts as *School Daze*.

I wonder if this film could be shot in chronological order. Most likely, it's not feasible. But it's an interesting thought.

With *Do The Right Thing* . . . no . . . even before, with *School*

Daze and *She's Gotta Have It,* we've started something. Young Black people are coming together, as one, to make our own films. It's never been done before on this scale. What we're doing is revolutionary and courageous. No other Black people in the industry are doing what we're doing. I'm not bragging, I'm just sorry it isn't being done by more folks.

If I'm dealing with the Black lower class, I have to acknowledge that the number one thing on folks' minds is getting paid. It's on everyone's mind, lower class or not, but the issue has more consequences when you're poor, flat broke, busted. Mookie's driving concern is money; how much and how to get it.

MOOKIE

I gots to get paid.

Mookie repeats this often. When he delivers pizzas, he refuses to leave until he gets a tip. You can believe that.

Mookie is an instigator, a rabble-rouser. He's a cantankerous person, always on the offensive. Mookie loves to start arguments. He should be arguing the entire movie. He's small but he has the mouth to back it up.

Spike, don't forget: A way to get Mookie out of the pizzeria is to have him make deliveries. This gets him out of the salt mines: Sal's Famous Pizzeria. Mookie has his female friends call the pizzeria to have pies delivered to their apartments.

One of the film's strongest relationships has to be between Mookie and his sister. (Sometime soon, Spike, you should find a name for her.) Our parents are not around, they probably passed. Ruby Dee's character is a mother figure to Joie's character and Ossie Davis is a father figure to Mookie.

Mookie and his sister love each other very much, but they go at it at times. She is bothered that Mookie—like many Black youths —has no vision. Mookie's sister constantly tells him he can't see beyond the next day, the end of his nose. It's the truth. The future might be too scary for kids like Mookie, so they don't think about it. They live for the present moment, because there is nothing they feel they can do about the future. What I'm really talking about is a feeling of helplessness, or powerlessness, that who you are and what effect you can have on things is absolutely nil, zero, jack shit, nada.

MOOKIE

Look Jade, why don't you leave me da hell alone.
I don't have a mother or father, so don't be
fronting like Mommy or Daddy. What do you want
me to do? Look I'm just a strugglin' Black man
trying to keep my dick hard . . .

JADE

Is that all you want in life—to keep ya dick
hard?

MOOKIE

No that's not all. I also want to get paid.

JADE

Yeah, you little $250 a week plus tips. That's
getting paid alright.

MOOKIE

Do you have ten dollars you can loan me?

Remember how in *Raging Bull,* jealousy was Jake La Motta's Achilles' heel? Well, for Mookie it's money, money, and mo' money. He is constantly counting his money, arranging the dollar bills so they face the same way. It's about being paid.

I was searching for a reason why Mookie should go back to Sal's Pizzeria the morning following the riot. Now I've got it. Mookie goes back there to find Sal because he wants to get paid. Mookie never got paid by check, always in cash, he's off da books.

Mookie gets paid.

In rehearsal with Richard Edson, Giancarlo Esposito, and
Danny Aiello: We had five rehearsal days for the eight-and-
a-half-week shoot. On day one, the entire cast met for a full
read-through, followed by an open discussion of the script.
The remaining four days we broke into small groups and
went over individual scenes.

The Corner Men in rehearsal (left to right): Paul Benjamin, Robin Harris, Frankie Faison.

The Corner Men on set.

At the premiere of *Midnight Run* with Robert De Niro and Danny Aiello (photo by Steve Sands).

My sister Joie rehearses with Giancarlo Esposito.

Brothers of the Fruit of Islam monitor the set: "We had to shut down two crack houses adjacent to the location before we started shooting. All hours of the day and night, cars would pull up in front of the crack houses and people would run in to cop drugs. We found spent M-16 cartridges while cleaning the abandoned buildings that were used as location sites. These crack dealers weren't to be taken lightly.

"We hired the Fruit of Islam as a security force at the beginning of set construction. Initially the brother in command wanted to bring out a hundred men to show force. There weren't that many residents on the block. If we brought out a hundred men, it would have looked like an army occupation. I convinced him that twenty was enough.

"I got a kick out of seeing the FOI brothers in bowties and suits walking around the set with their walkie-talkies. Early on we got a few inquiries from the police. I explained that the men in suits were our private security force. I didn't go into the fact that they were also Louis Farrakhan's army."—BRENT OWENS, LOCATION MANAGER

"When it comes to production design, Spike leaves the broader picture up to me, but he does get specific about details. The Mike Tyson mural, for example, he was very specific about this, to the point of being crazed. Midway through preproduction he decided he just had to have this mural, even though it wasn't originally budgeted for."
—WYNN THOMAS, PRODUCTION DESIGNER

The Posse (left to right): Steve White (Ahmad), Martin Lawrence (Cee), Christa Rivers (Ella), Leonard Thomas (Punchy): We had a hard time finding Ella. We needed someone who was "street," who talked loud, and didn't have a shy bone in her body. None of the women we auditioned came close to being Ella. Then I remembered Christa Rivers.

When I spoke at Howard University last year, I was heckled good-naturedly by a young woman who wanted to act in my films. Her name was Christa and she was a recent graduate of Duke Ellington High School for the Performing Arts in Washington, D.C. We tracked down Christa's number, but her phone was disconnected. It took two weeks to contact her. The day after we reached her, she took the train up from D.C. to audition in New York, and got the part.

Coproducer Monty Ross, Danny Aiello, Melvin Van Peebles, Ossie Davis (left to right): "Like Melvin, Spike is a writer, as well as a director and an actor. They're both fiercely independent. Because of the time period Melvin came along at, it seems his independence worked to his disadvantage. After having led the modern Black independent film movement into the seventies, he was blackballed by Hollywood for not wanting to play things their way. The way Melvin works is not traditional, the way he sees things is not traditional, and the studios didn't like that.

"Before starting *Do The Right Thing*, I worked with Melvin and his son Mario on their new film, *Identity Crisis*. Melvin did that film similar to the way he did his first film and like Spike did *She's Gotta Have It*—on an extremely low budget, with no upfront studio support, but with complete creative control.

"I think the difference between Melvin and Spike is that Spike would ideally like to have it both ways. Spike wants to keep his independence, but he also wants to be recognized, respected, and given his due by Hollywood; meaning mainly, given the budgets he needs to do his thing.

"Spike doesn't want to be an outsider as far as Hollywood is concerned. He's somewhat of a historian of film, Black film in particular. He doesn't want to fall into that same trap that many Black filmmakers have fallen into. It's been proven again and again that you can have the rug pulled out from under you at almost any point."—PRESTON HOLMES, PRODUCTION MANAGER

Me and Ernie D in Sal's Famous Pizzeria: "While we were shooting *School Daze,* Spike told me that the next film was gonna take place on the hottest day of the year. He said to keep in mind that the murder rate goes up in the summertime.

"I began to think about ways to portray heat visually, about what to do colorwise to reproduce the feeling of bright sun and relentless heat. I remember seeing *Lawrence of Arabia* when I was a kid. I must have visited the Coca-Cola stand three times before the film was over. I wanted that effect for *Do The Right Thing.*"—ERNEST DICKERSON

" 'Fight the Power,' the song you hear on Radio Raheem's box, wasn't ready in time for the shoot. It was a handicap working without the song, given that it was such an influence on this character's life. Try imagining music you've never heard before. I didn't want to do anything too rhythmic with my walk for fear of being off the beat. I didn't want to look like a white boy. Like Jerry Lewis, Radio Raheem Lewis!"—BILL NUNN

"In my original costume sketches, I put a Hawaiian shirt on Vito, Richard Edson's character. Then Danny Aiello came in for his fitting and announced that he wanted to wear a Hawaiian shirt. I gave Danny a Hawaiian shirt instead, and put Richard in something else.

"When Pino, John Turturro's character, comes to the pizza shop in the beginning of the film, he's in all black. You'd never know he works at a pizzeria. Then he changes to a white 'guinea' T-shirt for work. When the family closes up shop for the night, John changes back into the black outfit. Which is all meant to support his character's disdain for the work he does and the neighborhood."—RUTHE CARTER, COSTUME DESIGNER

"I became known as Smiley in the neighborhood. Some people knew that I was acting, some didn't. The kids around the block imitated the way I walked and talked, just like the kids do in the film. I had the rare opportunity to see how a person with a disability like Smiley's is treated."
—ROGER SMITH

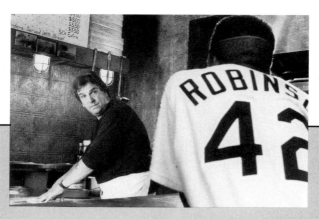

"Sal, may I get paid?" "With a contemporary film you can't really go to the library to do production design research. Instead I sent our location scout out to look for pizzerias that might serve as models for Sal's Famous.

"I knew that I wanted to use decorative sheet metal in the pizzeria. It has such a wonderful texture and is much more interesting than the walls that you normally find in pizzerias. As a designer, what I needed to do was find an existing pizzeria that looked similar to the one I wanted to design, so I wouldn't feel I wasn't making an inappropriate choice. We did find an old pizzeria in Coney Island with decorative sheet metal on the walls. Once I saw that, I breathed easier knowing I wasn't being totally farfetched."
—WYNN THOMAS

Sam Jackson (Mister Señor Love Daddy) and Ernest Dickerson on the set of We Love Radio: "The film takes place in one day and we had eight weeks of varying weather conditions to reproduce this one day. Lighting continuity was our toughest job. During preproduction we sat down and figured out the exact time, down to the minute, that each scene takes place so I could get a sense of how the light would change from scene to scene.

"Nighttime was another concern of mine. Often in New York, the heat is more oppressive at night. Since we don't have the sun at night, how do we show heat? Normally you use cool blue tones for nighttime, but I wanted to stay away from anything that suggested coolness. I decided to use yellows and reds, as if there was no moonlight, and all the light was coming from streetlamps. This added warmth."
—ERNEST DICKERSON

Turn on the johnny pump: "We talked about doing this film every possible way: as a union shoot, a nonunion shoot, or a combination of both. We talked about the possibility of shooting the film in another city. That was something that no one on our side wanted to do. It was suggested by the studio as a way of saving money. Universal even asked us to consider shooting on the back lot, so we wouldn't have to bank on eight weeks of beautiful sunny weather in New York. There were certain things that Spike didn't want to give up. And perhaps most important was that the film be shot in Brooklyn, on location in Bedford-Stuyvesant."
—JON KILIK, LINE PRODUCER

Blocking a shot with John, Danny, and Ernest: "The full-cast read-through was a weird experience for me. I didn't know most of the cast members. My character, Pino, says all these racist things. In fact, just saying the stuff out loud for the first time literally made me sick. I kept thinking, God, what have I got myself into?"—JOHN TURTURRO

Stevie Wonder stopped by the set one night to wish us well.

Brooklyn-born Willie Randolph (second from left), the great second baseman who now plays for the L.A. Dodgers, was another esteemed visitor. With him are Larry Cherry, our hairstylist, and Rosie Perez (Tina).

Ruby's last day: I've never seen a more loving married couple than Ruby Dee and Ossie Davis. I'm not trying to soup them up, it's just the truth. I'm sure they have their fights. Everybody fights. Ruby must have kicked him out of the house a few times. But really, it's great seeing two people who've been married for forty-something years still in love and working together.

Ossie Davis as Da Mayor: During one of our night shoots, we ran into a situation I always try to avoid—having the entire crew wait for an actor. It's better to pay one actor overtime and have him come an hour early, than have fifty grumbling crew members waiting for an actor to get to the set.

The actor we were waiting for in this case was Ossie Davis. It wasn't Ossie's fault. The assistant directors should have given him an earlier call time. Ossie was expected at 7:00 P.M. We were ready to shoot Ossie's scene at 6:45. Ossie's limousine pulls up to the set at 7:15. Ossie runs into his dressing room, throws on his costume, goes through makeup, and rushes to the set at 7:25. He goes straight to his mark, does three perfect takes, and he's finished for the night. What a professional!

Ossie is a great actor. I'm sure Ossie has regrets about the roles he wasn't offered or bitterness about the acclaim and money that should have been his. Every Black artist of his generation must have a measure of that.

Radio Raheem takes on the camera.

Danny Aiello is an opinionated guy, but he's a great actor, and he respects a director. Actors who have worked with me know I'm always open to suggestions. And if I don't think something will work, I give them my no immediately. I said plenty of no's to Danny. And what's wonderful about Danny is his feelings were never hurt. He didn't clam up. He'd say, 'Spike, you're right, that's a bad idea.' I did end up incorporating many of Danny's suggestions and we have a better film because of his insight.

Rosie Perez with the Toulson triplets. Travell (on Rosie's lap) played Tina and Mookie's son, Hector. His brothers were on standby.

Mookie's girl, Tina: "I went out to dinner with Diva Osorio, who plays my mother in the film. We talked for hours. I ended up telling her about my childhood and my own mother. Diva was slick. She used what I told her to get a rise out of me while we were shooting our scene together.

"In the scene, Tina asks her mother to babysit and she refuses. They argue and Tina's mother tells her off. In the last take, Diva said something in Spanish about going out with good-for-nothing niggers. For one minute I thought she was my real mother. I turned around and slammed the door in Diva's face. I really meant it. I was so pissed off, I started crying.

"I tripped back to all the painfulness of my teenage years, the constant confrontations with my mother, it all just came back on me. Spike called cut. We broke for lunch. I couldn't stop crying for the longest time. Even the assistant cameraman came over to ask if I was okay. I said, 'A few hours of therapy and I'll be fine!'"—ROSIE PEREZ

Mookie & Da Mayor: "Spike and the other young Black artists coming along make me feel like it's okay to die now. They've gone beyond where my generation was able to go as artists, as performers, as filmmakers. Something we did or said must have touched them. It's marvelously satisfying to know that your accomplishments encouraged others. What more could you ask for, than to see your children move beyond where you were able to go?"—RUBY DEE

"My family moved to Hollis, Queens, when I was six. I have fond memories of Hollis. It was a mixed neighborhood. None of my close friends were white. By the time my family moved, we were the only white people left on the block. We stayed in Queens, but we moved to a neighborhood called Rosedale, which was Irish and Italian. I was treated badly at first because I was darker than most of the kids. My mother still lives in Rosedale. It's predominantly Black now. The same thing happened. The white people just ran away."
—JOHN TURTURRO

Joie Lee (Jade) & Richard Edson: "I had questions about what kind of character Jade was and I took them to Spike. He told me that she walks the fence. Jade's in a grey area, not black or white, when it comes to politics. Instead of African accessories, I thought that Jade would have the generic American stuff that most of us have in our homes.

"Spike also told me that Jade worked in a department store. This helped me place her even further. Initially I thought Jade bought her furniture from the Salvation Army. Now I realized she could get brand-new items from the department store with her employee's discount. So that's how the design process begins. I find out as much as I can about characters and piece together their world."—WYNN THOMAS

Ella, Ahmad, Punchy, Da Mayor, and Cee (left to right): "When you get old in this country, you become a statue, a monument. And what happens to statues? Birds shit on them. There's got to be more to life for an elder than that! There should be an army of just elders. If there are wars to be fought, let the elders fight them. Elders should be far more politically active than young folks. We should be able to command respect, turn tables, and make things happen.

   "We're giving up something very precious when we abdicate our role as elders, when we go around snatching at youth. Youth has its time, middle age has its time, and so does being an elder. It has its ripeness and its beauty. And somehow we've got to make that sexy."—RUBY DEE

Radio Raheem's love and hate rings are my homage to *Night of the Hunter.*

John Savage as Clifton: Danny Aiello and I were at Columbus Restaurant one night and John Savage sat down at our table. Word had got back to John that the role of Clifton in *Do The Right Thing* was open. It didn't matter to John that it was a bit role and that there wasn't much money in it; he just wants to work.

We were forced to postpone shooting Clifton's scene a number of times because of bad weather. We were down to the wire. John was on his way to Africa to work on a film and he couldn't change his travel plans. Finally, the day before John was set to leave for Africa, we were able to squeeze in the shot.

It was John's idea that Clifton ride a bike and drink Tropicana. I gave him the Celtics T-shirt with Larry Bird's name and number. I have nothing personal against Larry Bird. He's a contemporary white American icon and I was commenting on that.

Clifton is a white homesteader who got tired of paying exorbitant rents in Manhattan and found a good deal on a house in Bed-Stuy. Clifton steps on Buggin' Out's sneakers by accident, but an apology isn't enough. Clifton realizes he's being tested: If he punks out, these kids will make his life on the block a living hell. On the other hand, Clifton doesn't want things to get physical because he'll get his butt kicked. To me this scene is really about how men, Black and white, test each other's manhood.

Richard Edson and John Turturro: "Spike wanted me to play Pino at first. For two months I did a lot of research on his type of character. Pino has a core of meanness, and I had to search deep to find this within myself. Then Spike told me that he switched my role to Vito, the good guy, and gave Pino to John Turturro. I had seen John's work before and I loved the guy. He's got all the bad-guy parts down pat. I'm not even in the running. I conceded gracefully.

"I still think if we had wanted to go against type, I should have played Pino. John is the dark Italian with the curly hair. He's rebelling against his physical similarities to the other race. It makes it too easy for the audience. Racism isn't about appearance, but how a person thinks about himself and reacts to the world. Often a racist will be someone who looks the least likely to be."—RICHARD EDSON

Jade and Mother Sister: "We've all known people who have what I call 'the negative love quotient.' Mother Sister is one of these. They love, but they can't let you know it and they can't show it. They care about you, they observe you, they want to be in your company, but they show it by dismissing you, making fun of you, or grabbing or snatching. An embrace embarrasses them and leaves them vulnerable. Their love is a backhanded kind of love."—RUBY DEE

Pino slurs Blacks: "You gold-teeth, gold-chain-wearing, fried-chicken-and-biscuit-eating, monkey, ape, baboon, big-thigh, fast-running, high-jumping, spear-chucking, 360-degree basketball-dunking, Tit soon, spade, Moulan Yan. Take your fucking piece of pizza and go the fuck back to Africa."

Sonny (Steve Park) slurs Jews: "It's cheap, I got a good price for you, Mayor Koch, 'How I'm doing?,' chocolate-egg-cream-drinking, bagel and lox, B'nai B'rith, Jew asshole."

Frank Vincent (Charlie) and Miguel Sandoval (Officer Ponte): I wanted Charlie, the character who gets his car drenched in the johnny pump, to be an Italian. I went to Martin Scorcese for suggestions. Marty mentioned Frank Vincent, whom he directed in *Raging Bull*. The first time I called Frank, he didn't know who I was. Frank called Scorcese and said, "Who is this guy Spike Lee? Is he Oriental?"

Radio Raheem and Buggin' Out in full effect.

"I was doing a play in Yugoslavia right before starting *Do The Right Thing*. I got back to New York on a Wednesday, and I was on camera for Spike by Friday. I didn't have much time to establish my look and my props.

"We chose to stay away from an overtly political look and went for something clean and nondescript. At one point Spike considered giving me a shopping cart. He ruled that out as it would read too much like a bag person. We decided that Smiley was taken care of by a sympathetic aunt or grandmother. He wasn't a transient or a homeless person.

"I was nervous my first day on camera because I still didn't know for sure what I was going to do with the cards printed with the photo of Malcolm and Martin, although the cards were ready for me. I was given a number of colored markers and I started coloring in the cards. So, that's how they came to be.

"One of the extras that day had a Walkman and it was purchased from him and given to me as a prop. It worked perfectly because it was an odd Walkman with a radio antenna that looks like an old transistor. I decided to always have the antenna up as if I was in constant communication with the ancestors."—ROGER SMITH

Cheesing with Richard Edson.

"Cut Creator" Barry Brown, editor of *School Daze* and *Do The Right Thing*, comes to the set to discuss the previous day's rushes.

Da Mayor saves Eddie Lovell (Richard Habersham) from being hit by a car: "During preproduction we scheduled a meeting for homeowners on the block. We went over our production schedule and discussed the improvements planned on several homes. Everyone seemed pleased that we were there. Shutting down the crack houses won us some points with the homeowners. They were much more willing to lease us their property after we did that.

"One crack house, which was on Lexington Street, was notorious. The place was foul: crack vials, dead animals, used condoms, and feces everywhere. The straw that broke the camel's back was seeing a woman with two children no older than three, and an infant in a carriage, go into the crack house and stay for twenty minutes or so. We sealed the place up the next day."—BRENT OWENS

Mother Sister always watches: "Young as Spike is, I didn't expect him to remember a character like Mother Sister, who is straight out of my childhood. That proves that the character persists. Mother Sister still lives in the neighborhood. She hears everything and sees everything. And she's still an integral part of the community, especially a community that's healthy."—RUBY DEE

"When I sat down to read the script for the first time, I opened to page one and saw the word *pizzeria*. I nearly put the damn thing down. For me, *pizzeria* immediately brings to mind the worst stereotypes of Italians. It's like sticking a watermelon in a Black man's hand—he's gonna say, 'I ain't playing this fucking part.' But I sat back and read on. I ended up loving the script. I saw the possibilities of it being an important film."—DANNY AIELLO

Frank Stettner gives neighborhood kids an introduction to sound recording: "Most Hollywood films, even independent films, don't give a goddamn about the neighborhoods they film in. They have permits and the police behind them. They stage a military occupation of a block for a couple of days, then they pack up and leave their garbage.

"I know for sure that the crew and cast of *Do The Right Thing*, from the craft service people on up, cared about the people on Stuyvesant Street. We organized a clothing drive, we gave away food, we hired people from the neighborhood. In a very concrete way, we did what we could."—GIANCARLO ESPOSITO

"I tried to talk to people on the set about race relations on a number of occasions, but no one was too interested. It's funny, because here we were doing a movie about the subject, and we couldn't even talk about it amongst ourselves."—RICHARD EDSON

"One intense scene was the final confrontation in the pizzeria, when Radio Raheem, Smiley, and I return to have it out with Sal. We did a lot of ad-libbing. I got the ball rolling when I called Sal a guinea bastard. Danny paused. I saw the shock on his face. He was really taken aback. I liked him, he liked me, but we had to separate at that moment. I could hear a bell go off in his head. I could hear him say to himself, 'I don't like this kid. I don't like this fucking kid at all.'

"Things got personal at that point. They had to. When Danny called me a nigger, of course I hated it, but I've been called that all my life. I'm much more used to being called a nigger than Danny is to being called a guinea bastard."
—GIANCARLO ESPOSITO

"Some people are convinced that movies are real life. They come up to me on the subway and ask, 'Aren't you the guy who killed so and so?'

"Many of the people that recognize me as an actor are Black. Hopefully they'll know that *Do The Right Thing* is just a movie, and that I'm nothing like the character Pino. Spike tried to allay my fears about this, but people are bound to hate this character and identify me with him. As long as Spike gets me on the cover of *Ebony* with him, I'll be okay!

"Seriously, you've got to take chances like that as an actor. I'm not interested in playing heroes, because I know in real life I'm a good person. The nature of drama is conflict. Leading-man roles bore me. I need a character I can sink my teeth into."—JOHN TURTURRO

The riot is too much for Mother Sister: "Ossie and I both look at being Black as an enormously exciting way to spend your life on this earth. We can't imagine not being Black. What would we do with ourselves? When we talk about where we belong, we know we belong to Black people. It's proven true in our lives. We will never go without a job. We can always go among our people and there'll be work for us."—RUBY DEE

"I wanted to do something literal to make Buggin' Out live up to his name. I got this idea of wearing glasses that would make my eyes look very big. I brought the idea to Spike. He was worried that glasses would make me look too much like Big Brother Almighty from *School Daze*, but he was willing to check them out.

"It cost me $275 to let Spike see the glasses. I had a pair made that magnified my eyes five times, then I was fitted for contacts to reverse the prescription of the glasses. My equilibrium just went out the window at first. It took me a while to build up a tolerance.

"I showed up at the first day of rehearsal wearing the glasses. No one said anything, they just looked at me funny. They must have thought my eyes had gone bad, but were too polite to mention it. On the second day I was convinced that no one noticed. I was crushed. Eventually I asked Spike what he thought. He said, 'They're fine. I thought your eyes looked kinda big.' "—GIANCARLO ESPOSITO

Radio Raheem, Smiley, and Buggin' Out: "None of us knew that my character Smiley would be as aggressive as he became. The scene that set the stage was when I knock on the pizzeria's window and Pino comes outside to tell me to get the hell away. This part of the scene was totally improvised. The first couple of takes I meekly walked away. By the last take, something else was happening inside of me. I wanted to respond to Pino with the same anger he was putting out, and I did.

"According to the script, when the fight breaks out in the pizzeria, Smiley hides under a table. But after we shot that scene between Smiley and Pino, Spike decided to have Smiley actively involved in the climax of the film. So Smiley became the person who sets the pizzeria on fire."—ROGER SMITH

"Seeing your best friend die no doubt changes your entire life. I don't think Buggin' Out realized that the mess he started would go as far as it did. He probably thought that a picture of a Black person would go on the wall of Sal's Famous, and the issue would be settled.

"I don't think that what happens to Buggin' Out is resolved. That's another picture. I think a lot of it is another picture as far as Spike Lee endings go. The other picture is in your brain. You must resolve it youself."—GIANCARLO ESPOSITO

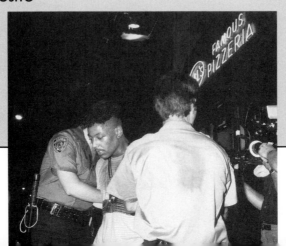

Cops apply the infamous Michael Stewart choke hold to
Radio Raheem. Yet another black man killed at the hands of
the police.

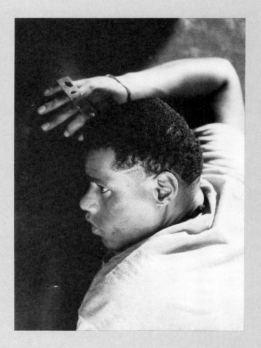

Murdered by hate.

Sal's burns: "I grew up on a farm in the South. Sometimes I'd get the devil in me, and I'd chase cats and puppies, but cats in particular. You can chase a cat all day long. But if you corner him, it's like taking your life into your own hands. Because that cat is going to come out of the corner with a vengeance.

"Perhaps it's not a terrific analogy in respect to Black people in America. But I do see that kind of anger in us. And rightfully so. I've experienced it. I have survived in this business. Not too many people know what it has taken for me to survive under the circumstances for as long as I have. And I have not survived without anger."—PAUL BENJAMIN

Chanting "Coward Beach": "Racism is a crusher. That we have survived this long in the face of such concerted assaults on our psyches is a miracle. The question is, how do we let our children know what has happened to us, and what continues to happen, without turning them into cynics and haters? We can't buy the lies of the enemy, but we also have to recognize our friends."—RUBY DEE

Pino: "Fuckin' niggers."

3:00 A.M.

Take your pick: Montgomery, Alabama, 1963—or Brooklyn,
New York, 1989?

"As far as I could see, there was no real racial antagonism during the riot scene, just good acting. Though I bet there was a lot going on in people's heads. There have been times in all of our lives when we wanted to have a fight like this with a person of another race. Or times that we wanted to say the negative things that were said."—MARTIN LAWRENCE

Danny, his son and stunt double, Danny Aiello, Jr., John Turturro, and Martin Lawrence (left to right): "It was a jovial set, even during the riot scene. Martin kept us laughing throughout. Danny made him do his impersonations about 150 times. The poor guy was burnt out. He'll never be the same again. 'Martin, Martin,' Danny would say, 'One more time. Do Sugar Ray Leonard.'"
—JOHN TURTURRO

"Spike didn't tell me he wanted me to do a monologue in front of Yes-Jesus Baptist Church until the morning we shot it. It wasn't scripted, so I asked Spike what he had in mind. He said, 'I don't know, you're the character, what would you say?'

"I listened, as I always did, to Smiley's tape of Malcolm X delivering his 'Ballot or the Bullet' speech. Malcolm has a line about how George Washington traded a Black man for a keg of molasses. Basically he's talking about the hypocrisy of American history.

"I kept repeating the line about the keg of molasses; to Smiley this is a fantastic fact. Smiley is one of those people who snatches bits of history and they become fantastic legendary ideas to him. Like the fact that Mike Tyson sent his boxing gloves to Nelson Mandela to help fight apartheid. Eventually the monologue came together."
—ROGER SMITH

Watching Sal's burn.

Sal's Famous Pizzeria, R.I.P.

"When we met for the first time to talk over the script, I told
Spike, 'You may be a little to the left of the leftest guy
I know, and I'm 150 miles to the right of Ronald Reagan.
Can we work together'?"—DANNY AIELLO

The *Do The Right Thing* crew: "This was Spike's first time out with a union crew. Going union has some positive and negative sides. Theoretically, it means you're getting the skilled and experienced professionals, and that's positive. The drawback is there are few Black technicians in the film unions.

"There were more Black technicians on this film than you would find on any other union production being done in New York. We were given some concessions from the union to allow us to use nonunion Black technicians in place of union people, because there were no minority people in the union in these categories."—PRESTON HOLMES

It's a wrap.

Sal can't believe Mookie has the gall to ask for his money. Sal doesn't want to hear it. His business has been burnt down to the ground and this guy Mookie wants to get paid. The dialogue isn't there yet, but that's definitely the final scene.

About the riot. As the crowd torches the pizzeria, the Fire Department arrives on the scene. Before firemen turn their hoses on the fire, they direct the water toward the people to disperse them. So we're back to Montgomery and Birmingham, Alabama; the only thing missing is Bull Connor and the German shepherds.

I had written earlier about a torrential downpour that comes at the height of the uprising. Now I have this idea about the crowd getting hosed. When I don't read my notes, I miss making these connections. Alright, alright, I'm gonna read all my notes tonight.

FEBRUARY 17, 1988

This morning I was on WOL radio in Washington, D.C. The control room is in a storefront, so folks on the street can look right in. That's exactly what I want for We Love, the radio station in *Do The Right Thing*. We Love—Home of the Voice of Choice, Mister Señor Love Daddy, the world's only twelve-hour strong man. Giancarlo Esposito might be the Voice of Choice for Mister Señor Love Daddy. Giancarlo could do it as a Black/Puerto Rican thing.

The first shot of the film will be an extreme closeup of Mister Señor Love Daddy looking directly into the camera. He says, "Wake up," then the camera pulls back through the window storefront to reveal the station, We Love, then cranes up to reveal the entire block where the film will take place. Vicious.

MISTER SEÑOR LOVE DADDY

Here I am, am I here. Y'know it, it you know.
This is Mister Señor Love Daddy
doing the nasty to your ears, your
ears to the nasty. I play only the platter dat
matter, da matters dat platter.

This should be Mister Señor Love Daddy's speech pattern. He yings and yangs, flops and flips.

MISTER SEÑOR LOVE DADDY

I get paid stupid dollar to make da females scream and holla'.

When the uprising is taking place, Mister Señor Love Daddy should describe the events as if he were commentating a championship boxing match.

MISTER SEÑOR LOVE DADDY

Here we are in Brooklyn and the folks are going off. It's unbelievable, unbelievable. I haven't seen the likes of this since the blackout of '77. Oh my, a garbage can just went through the sky. It's getting ugly. If more of this goes on I'm outta here.

I'm guilty of concerning myself with casting before I've completed the script, but I can't resist. Bill Nunn would be a more appropriate Mister Señor Love Daddy than Giancarlo Esposito.

I need to fly down to Florida and talk to Jack the Rapper. He's the dean of all Black radio jocks. Jack the Rapper is down for the cause and he has all the old-time lingo. That's the stuff I need for this film.

FEBRUARY 20, 1988

Yesterday this girl asked me to sign an autograph for her and address it to Mookie. That's strange, a girl nicknamed Mookie.

The entire month of March I'll be immersed in *Do The Right Thing*. This is all I'm gonna do or think about. To use an expression of Wynton Marsalis's, I'm gonna be shedding, as in the woodshed.

Do The Right Thing has to be ninety minutes. That's it, ninety minutes. We're gonna be moving when we shooting this mutha, moving fast. It will be like *She's Gotta Have It* in that sense. I still have to decide whether it would be better to have five- or six-day weeks.

I thought I was through with traveling and promoting *School Daze*. The film goes to five more markets this week, and I'm being asked to visit these cities. I wanted to start writing the script on March 1, but if I go on this tour I won't be back in Nueva York until March 5. I have to decide today whether I'll go or not. I'm tired of talking about *School Daze*. Like it or not, the fact remains, I'm the selling point in this film.

FEBRUARY 21, 1988

It's 8:30 P.M. and I have finally read my notes to date. It's about time, Spike. You've got to stop bullshitting. I have lots of material —plenty of good stuff that I had forgotten about.

Certain themes keep popping up in my notes, which is a good sign. I must remember the line Sal always repeats, THIS IS AMER-ICA. It's key.

I should write in a group of wild and crazy kids. They wreak havoc throughout the film. In one scene they throw water balloons out of a window.

There will definitely be a Puerto Rican influence in this film. I want to hear some Spanish. No subtitles, though. I like that barrage of Spanish, punctuated with two or three words of English, that comes out when somebody is mad.

DIALOGUE

Ya ass is so broke, you're thirty cents from a quarter.

We have to use Robin Harris in this film. I wouldn't dare to write his dialogue. I would just set it up, give him the ball, and let him run. Robin could be part of a group of men that hangs out on the corner all day, drinking beer, signifying, and playing the dozens.

You always see brothers like this out on the corner. Accompanying Robin Harris could be Sam Jackson and Frankie Faison.

There's a paragraph from *The Autobiography of Malcolm X* that talks about the passivity of Black Americans. I'd like to preface the script with that quote.

I'm still deciding about whether to include some stuff about drugs. I haven't addressed the issue before on film. Not to acknowledge that drugs exist might be a serious omission in this film. The drug epidemic is worse than the plague. Entire generations are being wiped out by drugs. If drugs aren't getting them, then the guys shooting over the drugs are. My goal is to show how the different social pressures that lead to this are all connected.

That's it, I've decided. I'm not going out on the road anymore. I'll devote all my time and energies to *Do The Right Thing*. Columbia can kiss my black ass, two times. If they had their way, I'd be on the road the rest of my life promoting this film.

After *School Daze* I can understand why people don't read reviews. Unless you're strong to the T, reviews can have an effect on you. I'm not talking about making you mad. I'm talking about how reading reviews can influence your thinking. You could end up making the film they want you to make instead of following your original vision. It's dangerous and that's exactly why I've stopped reading them.

Even though the criticism of *School Daze* is putting me through the fire, I can tell you now this is nothing compared to what the next film is gonna get.

Yesterday Monty, Arthur Klein, and I sat down again to brainstorm about *Do The Right Thing*. We're definitely leaning towards Paramount.

FEBRUARY 28, 1988

Yesterday I began work on the script. Well, actually, I began the last work before the actual writing of the script. I put down all the ideas or scenes and dialogue on three-by-five index cards. TOMOR-ROW, I'll begin to write this motherfucker.

This morning I got up early to go to my corner store, T and T, to buy the paper. The young guys who work there had a Run-D.M.C. tape on. The owner, an old Italian guy, says, "What da fuck is dat? Turn that jungle music off. We're not in Africa. It's giving me a stomach ache." Sooner or later it comes out. Okay, so you don't like rap music. But why does it have to be about jungle music and Africa? I should have Sal say the same words to Radio Raheem in the movie.

FEBRUARY 29, 1988

It's the last day of February and I'm exactly where I want to be. I'm in a creative mood. I've finished making my three-by-five cards outlining every scene. March, the month I was born in, begins tomorrow. I'm ready and fired up.

MARCH 5, 1988

Last night I went to see Michael Jackson perform at Madison Square Garden. *School Daze* opened in ten more markets today. I had two hours of phone interviews this morning. It's 3:00 P.M. now and I haven't done any actual writing on the script. Instead, I read over what I wrote yesterday.

When I stopped writing today I was up to page 48, that's roughly twenty-four typed pages. That's almost a third of the script down and this is only the fifth day of writing. I'm pleased with myself. I'm not trying to rush through this stuff either.

I have the next forty or so scenes on index cards lined up in order. I need to keep Mookie in the forefront. But, I can't forget about his sister Jade, and, I have to include Mookie's woman, the one he does the ice cube number with.

This weekend has been great. I've been writing my butt off. I'm not gonna take any more days off, just write straight through to the end.

MARCH 8, 1988

I'm into my second week of writing and I'm halfway through the first draft. I feel good about it. I have at least two or three more drafts coming, but the first one I can go to Paramount Pictures with. It's also the draft I can show to Bob De Niro and my key production staff. I hope to go to Cannes and I can work on a second draft there.

Now that I'm halfway through, I can focus on Mookie's thing about getting paid. I have to keep in mind how the change from day to dusk then night affects what's happening in the story. In the summer, though, it really doesn't get dark till eight o'clock or so.

MARCH 10, 1988

I wrote like a madman yesterday from 7:00 A.M. to noon. In the evening I went to see the Knicks lose to the Lakers.

When I stopped writing I was on page 111, which is something like fifty-five typewritten pages. That's great considering I haven't been at it for a full two weeks yet. There's no doubt in my mind now that a crisp, lean, and mean ninety-page script will be ready in time for us to shoot in August. Monty and I should sit down now and start assembling a production staff.

MARCH 11, 1988

Monty and I went to a United Negro College Fund dinner for Michael Jackson last night. I sat on the dais between Yoko Ono and Valerie Simpson. All the UNCF presidents were there, as well as Dr. Keith, the current president of Morehouse, and Hugh Gloster, the former president who refused to allow us to shoot *School Daze* on the campus. Ossie Davis was the Master of Ceremonies and fired the place up.

The UNCF presidents gave us their support. They recognize what we're up against in getting features off the ground and they understand what we're trying to do with film. We're on the path. Like Mama told me just this morning, TRUTH CRUSHED TO EARTH SHALL RISE AGAIN. There it is, there it is.

MARCH 13, 1988

It's early Sunday morning, a week before my birthday. Today begins my third week on the first draft of *Do The Right Thing*. I should finish by the end of this week.

There is a book-signing Friday for *Uplift the Race* in New York. After that, I go straight to L.A. to a book-signing there and a birthday party for me that our publicist Pat Tobin is throwing. EU, the go-go band that performed in *School Daze,* is flying in from D.C. to perform. It's turning into a big thing.

Friday night I had dinner with Matt Dillon. We had a good time talking. I'm considering him to play one of the sons.

MARCH 14, 1988

Yesterday I let Lisa Jones read what I have written so far. She was laughing a lot, so that's a good sign. When I stopped writing I was on page 144; roughly seventy-two typewritten pages. I'm up to the point where the uprising begins. I'll finish before I go to Los Angeles this Friday.

I gotta watch it, the ending I'm talking about. I can't let the last scene between Mookie and Sal be too chummy. Remember, Sal has had his business burnt to the ground. Also, what are Sal, Vito, and Pino gonna do when the pizzeria goes up in flames? Do they stand there and watch or what? Think about it, Spike, think about it.

MARCH 15, 1988

I didn't write yesterday. I was too sleepy, but I did wake up at six this morning and I'm about to bust it out. Y'know the deal.

MARCH 17, 1988

Tuesday morning I finished the first draft of *Do The Right Thing*. It came in at roughly eighty-seven typed pages. It's the fastest script I have ever written. In all, the actual writing of the first draft took fifteen days, but I have been taking notes since December.

The first draft may be finished, but that doesn't mean my work is done. More work is still to come on script. I have three or four more drafts. Typewritten, it might be four or five pages less than ninety. We hope to start shooting on the first of August, a little over four months from now. Time is not to be wasted.

MARCH 26, 1988

Yesterday I picked up my scripts from the typist. I had only ten copies made. The only people who have read it so far are Monty and Lisa Jones. Of course y'know Lisa would break it down. Her biggest concern was that, as it is now, Sal is too nice to Mookie at the beginning of the final scene. Mookie instigated the burning of his pizzeria. This was his life and Sal should be mad as shit. Also, Sal's line about going to the beach has to go.

In this month's *Esquire* there is a great article by Pete Hamill about the plight of the Black underclass in America. We're really fucked up. This script should reflect that.

Mookie's girlfriend Tina is one of the thousands of teenage Black girls who has a child, but is still a child herself. Mookie is the father. I want an unknown young woman, maybe someone who's not an actress, to play Tina. I need a real live Ghetto Babe.

Tina always hounds Mookie for money.

TINA

Mookie, I need some money.

MOOKIE

I gave you a hundred bucks a week ago.

TINA

That was a week ago. Dat money has been gone.

Tina, who is seventeen or eighteen, lives with her mother. Tina's mom hates Mookie. She doesn't speak to him, just gives him dirty looks.

Now that Mookie has a child, of course his sister Jade is gonna be on his case. Even though Mookie is older than Jade, she's much more responsible and mature.

I'm gonna make a conscious effort to beef up my female characters in this script.

MARCH 26, 1988

Last night I was uptown. EU performed two shows at the Apollo. I tell ya, it is another world in Harlem. Black people up there are different from Brooklyn folks. They have their own style of dress and wear gold for days. It was good being there. I need to do it more often. It gives me material for future films.

MARCH 29, 1988

IMAGE

A phone receiver off the hook, swinging wildly from a telephone booth.

I've thumbed through the script, but haven't read it in its entirety since it was typed. So far, I've given scripts to:

1. Bill Horburg, Paramount Pictures

2. Casting director Robi Reed

3. Production designer Wynn Thomas

4. Ossie Davis & Ruby Dee

5. Monty Ross

6. Ernest Dickerson

I have a lunch date today with Bob De Niro. I'll give him the script. It's gonna be murder, waiting to see if he'll do it. I've never been in this situation before, asking a star of his magnitude. All I can do is hope for the best.

MARCH 30, 1988

I gave Bob De Niro the script at lunch. We left it at that, no promises, no nothing. He said he would get back to me soon. That's all, no mo', no less. Y'know Bob's gonna be straight.

I had a conference call with Bill Horborg and Teddy Zee, of Paramount Pictures, to go over some points in the script. Teddy is in New York at the Ritz-Carlton. After the call I went up there and we talked some more. Paramount is scared that this film might incite Black folks to riot. Needless to say, I don't agree with them.

I met this babe at my birthday party in L.A. at Funky Reggae. She was dancing atop a speaker, then she got on the dance floor and was killin'. I mean killin'. This babe can dance. I mean vicious. The next day Sugar Bear, EU's lead singer, told me she was from Brooklyn. Monty gave her our number. She called the other day.

Thank you Jesus. Her name is Rosie Perez. Not only is she from Brooklyn, she's from Fort Greene, my neighborhood. Help me, Jesus. I'm seriously considering her for the role of Tina. She's definitely what I'm looking for: a fine young ghetto babe. Rosie is Puerto Rican, but she looks Black. I know it's early, but I'm stuck on her for the role of Tina. We talked on the phone again last night.

APRIL 5, 1988

Yesterday we heard from Bob De Niro. He passed on the script. He said he's done roles like Sal before and doesn't want to repeat. He did however turn me on to a guy who he feels is perfect for the role of Sal. The guy, he says, once owned a pizzeria on Mulberry Street in Little Italy.

I have to decide whether we're gonna go for a star to play Sal or a strong, but relatively unknown, actor. I'm hesitant to go after another big name after Bob De Niro turned us down. Besides, our budget may not allow for it.

The actors I've sent scripts to so far are Matt Dillon, Richard Edson, Ossie Davis, and Ruby Dee. Yesterday we had interviews with a production manager, Preston Holmes, and a location scout, Grant Reid.

Paramount is getting shaky. I might have to fly out to L.A. next week. They keep suggesting I change the ending. The riot scene scares them. They want Mister Señor Love Daddy to be the last person we see in the film. Hell no. The last scene has to be between Mookie and Sal. The script is still a first draft, but the basic structure is fine the way it is. I won't allow my work to be altered to such a degree.

Paramount Pictures might not be the place to make this film. If it isn't, then let's find out as soon as possible and stop fucking around.

Question. Where do we go next? Touchstone, Orion, Universal? In a way all these motherfuckers are the same. However, going back to Columbia would be suicide, they failed to promote *School Daze* properly. (Steely Dawn wouldn't want me back, she's glad I'm gone.)

I've been taking notes, but I haven't started the second draft yet. First, I'd like to know where we're gonna be studiowise.

APRIL 6, 1988

Things are deteriorating with Paramount. I think they're afraid of making this picture. It's TOO BLACK, TOO STRONG. Ned Tannen, the president, has big problems with the end of the picture, especially Sal's line about Blacks being smarter because they don't burn down their own houses anymore. I gotta keep moving.

APRIL 9, 1988

A lot has happened these past few days. I've been in discussions with Paramount Pictures about the ending. They want an ending that they feel won't incite a giant Black uprising. They are convinced that Black people will come out of the theaters wanting to burn shit down.

I was totally discouraged with Paramount and practically broke off the talks. Bill Horborg called back the next day to say there has to be an ending that can satisfy myself and Paramount. So I'm flying out to L.A. to talk to Ned Tannen this Tuesday.

I sent a script to Jeffrey Katzenberg at Touchstone Pictures. It may have been hasty. We shall see. Jeffrey still feels he was jerked around on *School Daze;* he wanted the picture, and was ready to do the deal, but we went with Columbia. I would prefer Paramount to Touchstone, but hey!

D I A L O G U E

Ain't that some shit?

Yesterday we gave Rosie Perez a ride back from D.C. I can't think of a better person to play Mookie's girlfriend than Rosie. The thing about Rosie is her intelligence. She is from the street and knows the street. We'll read other people, but right now, Rosie Perez is my choice for Tina.

If we do use Rosie, then I'll write Tina as Puerto Rican. Tina's mother, who can't speak English, hates Mookie. This is great. Tina, Puerto Rican; Mookie, Black; and their kid's name is Angel.

APRIL 12, 1988

Yesterday we shot a TV spot for Jesse Jackson's presidential campaign. Monty and I put a crew together who donated their time and we shot the spot in one day. We're in a hurry to edit because the spot has to air this Thursday before the New York primary. That's why I'm not on my way to Los Angeles this morning. I'll go Saturday morning.

Yesterday morning I got a call from Jeffrey Katzenberg at Touchstone. He passed on *Do The Right Thing*. He said it's too small a picture for seven to ten million. He said maybe for three or four million.

APRIL 14, 1988

It's been a month since I finished the first draft of *Do The Right Thing* and I haven't picked it up since. It's time to start cranking out a second draft. We want to start preproduction on June 1. That gives us eight weeks before shooting begins on August 1.

Larry Fishburne read the script. Fish has decided that he no longer wants to play supporting roles after *School Daze*. He feels he's a leading man now. I don't agree with him, but if he feels it's in his best interest, I'm all for him.

Knowing that Fishburne won't be down with this film means it's time to juggle. I'll move Bill Nunn—who was Mister Señor Love Daddy—to Radio Raheem, Sam Jackson to Love Daddy, and Giancarlo Esposito to Buggin' Out.

DIALOGUE

Get a life
Ya simple Black bastard
Wake ya Monkey Ass up.

APRIL 16, 1988

I'm on a five-hour flight to Los Angeles. Before we took off, I read Jim Jarmusch's new script *One Night in Memphis*. There are similarities between our scripts. I like the form he uses. It's three interwoven stories that take place in a rundown hotel in Memphis, Tennessee. Jim is giving a role to my brother Cinque, which is good. It means Cinque can't work on my film, but it's better that he get a chance to act for Jim.

Yes yes, y'all, it's time to write the second draft of *Do The Right Thing*. There are a few critical points I have to expand:

1. The relationship between Mookie and Tina.

2. The relationship between Mookie and Radio Raheem.

3. How ML and Sweet Dick Willie rank on Coconut Sid about being West Indian.

4. Tina has to be introduced earlier. I'd like to do it by showing Tina, her child, and her mother, but not let it be known right away that Tina is Mookie's girlfriend.

5. I want to pay homage to *Night of the Hunter*. You know those brass-knuckle name rings that kids are wearing now? They're gold-plated and spread across four fingers. Radio Raheem will wear two of these. The one on his left hand will read "L-O-V-E," on his right, "H-A-T-E," just like Robert Mitchum's tattoos in *Night of The Hunter*. Radio Raheem tells Mookie a story about the rings that will be a variation on Robert Mitchum's tale of his tattoos. Vicious.

One of the problems of the ending of the film as it stands is that Mookie is too impartial when the riot breaks out. He has to be on

Radio Raheem's side from the beginning, even if he doesn't get physically involved.

I want to stay away from still photographs for the opening credits. I used stills in *She's Gotta Have It* and *School Daze*. I have been thinking about credits written in white chalk on a city street. Black asphalt. We could shoot them with a Louma crane.

APRIL 18, 1988

I had my long-awaited meeting with the big cheeses of Paramount Pictures, Ned Tannen, Gary Luchiesi, Teddy Zee, and Bill Horborg. It was a good meeting. I spoke passionately about the film. I felt I won over Ned Tannen, Teddy Zee, and Bill Horborg. It was another story with Gary. They meet tomorrow morning to decide whether the film will be done at Paramount. I feel, as does Bill Horborg, that they'll want to do it, but for eight million, not ten.

APRIL 20, 1988

I was supposed to hear from Paramount yesterday. Bill Horburg called me last night. Ned Tannen wants to take one more day to look at the script. Bill said again they might just do it for the right price, the right price being eight million or less. If it comes to that, I'm gonna have to jump at it. The important thing is that I continue to make films and keep the momentum going.

Paramount just called. Now they say they need until Monday to answer. I'm not getting nervous, though. One thing in our favor is the Writer's Guild strike. The studios need films. If they don't have product, they will have holes in their schedule. In the meantime, I have to look at some other places besides Paramount.

Arthur Klein and I have put Universal and Orion up next. Today I called Sam Kitt at Universal, he's in the acquisitions department. Yes, I have to keep my options open. It's important that I follow up *School Daze* right away. This is crucial, no recent Black filmmaker has been able to go from film to film like the white boys do.

I'm in Kansas City, Missouri, waiting for a connecting flight to Los Angeles. For the second weekend in a row, Paramount has yet to give us a word. I've been told we'll get it this Friday. We shall see.

I have a busy week coming up. We're shooting a video for Steel Pulse and a video for "I Can Only Be Me," the song Keith John sings in *School Daze*. And yes, I still have to finish the second draft of *Do The Right Thing*.

APRIL 25, 1988

A lot happened yesterday. Paramount Pictures called, they decided not to do the film. I kinda figured that, they were taking too long. Bill Horburg fought for me till the end. But he's not Ned Tannen. Just when I thought it was all sewn up with Paramount. Goes to show you, take nothing for granted, till the check is in the bank and has cleared.

Universal wants to do the film. By luck Sam Kitt, who I've known since *She's Gotta Have It,* is now at acquisitions for Universal. He's only been there for six weeks. Kitt saw the article on *Do The Right Thing* in *Variety* and gave me a call. He and Sean Daniels, another Universal honcho, came by my hotel when I was in L.A. last weekend. I gave them the script on a lark. Good thing I did, because about the same time, Paramount was giving me the axe.

The next day Sam came back to my hotel room to say Universal wants to do the film. Arthur Klein spoke to Sean Daniels on the phone yesterday and told him what we wanted to clinch the deal.

I know this project is getting close because I'm starting to dream about it. That's always a good sign for me.

APRIL 26, 1988

Danny Aiello is now my first choice for Sal. Richard Edson knows him and talked to him about the project. Last night Danny himself called. He's in Toronto doing *January Man* for Norman Jewison. He seemed excited about *Do The Right Thing*. I'm gonna send him a script today. My other choices are Joe Pesci and Joe Montagna. Shit, everybody's named Joe.

If we have to settle for a lower budget with Universal, then this film will have to get made nonunion. The question is, will the Teamsters fuck with us, and will the other film unions too? I'm banking on the fact that if we shoot it in the heart of Black Brooklyn, the unions won't have the balls to start some shit.

DIALOGUE

I'll put a Mike Tyson—ass beating on ya.

Remember to get Mike Tyson's picture in it, somehow. A poster, maybe.

Arthur Klein made a great suggestion today. For some reason I picked the first of August as the starting date to shoot. This film has to be shot in the heat of the summer. If we start the first of August, that gives us five weeks in August and five in September. Arthur says we should start in the middle of July. If we start preproduction on May 30, and shooting on July 18, that will still give us seven weeks of preproduction. This is the move, this is the move. This gives us only three-and-a-half weeks of shooting in September. I likes, I likes.

APRIL 28, 1988

I'm on a flight to Cleveland, Ohio, where I'll be speaking tonight at Kent State. Things are happening fast now for *Do The Right Thing*. Arthur Klein had a second conversation with Universal. He talked to Fred Bernstein, head of business affairs. Universal agreed to everything that we asked for except owning the negative. Two things that we'll end up haggling over and I won't budge on are mutual agreement on cast and final cut.

I'm gonna use Jon Kilik as a line producer, for the daily operation of the production. He's been doing the budget. The first one he did was all-union. Now he's doing a nonunion budget. This has to go out to Universal as soon as possible. I told Jon to have the budget come out to $7.5 million in total. That's all the money Universal is gonna give us.

Jon is preparing a nonunion budget, but it is still to be decided whether this will be a union or nonunion film. Ernest is concerned that a nonunion shoot in New York will get us in trouble with the unions and the Teamsters.

Yesterday I had dinner with my sister Joie. We had a good talk. I told her that she's in the film and she was very happy. We really need to talk more often than we do. I'm gonna build the role of Jade.

When Jade is giving Mookie a hard time, the one thing she mentions over and over is, "You're not responsible. You don't take care of your responsibilities." Mookie wants to know what responsibilities she is referring to. Jade says, "I didn't stutter. You don't take care of your responsibilities. Y'know what I'm talking 'bout." Of course we find out later, responsibilities means Mookie's child.

The name of the company for this film will be Da Moulan Yan Picture Company.

Robi Reed and Ruthe Carter are both working on Keenen Wayans's film *I'm Gonna Git You Sucka*. When I was in L.A. last weekend I met with Ruthe to talk about the problems we had on *School Daze* and how we could make things go smoother on *Do The Right Thing*. Despite our little conflicts, the costumes looked good on *School Daze*.

The question remains. Who's gonna play Sal, owner of Sal's Famous Pizzeria? It's been the million-dollar question for a while now. Monday night I talked to Danny Aiello on the phone. He hasn't received the script I sent him yet, U.S. customs held it up at the border. Danny says he'll call once he gets the script, and when he returns from Toronto we'll hook up.

Matt Dillon is shaky. I haven't heard from him. If Danny says yes, Matt will do the film as well. Richard Edson told me he'll talk to Matty. If that doesn't work, James Russo is a possibility, but that would require a switch, with Russo playing Pino and Edson as Vito. But let's not be hasty. Matty still might come around. Sal, Vito, and Pino—Danny Aiello, Richard Edson, and Matt Dillon.

MAY 2, 1988

I'm at Restaurant Florent waiting to have dinner with Sam Kitt of Universal Pictures. He's in New York a couple a days before he heads out to Cannes.

Monty and I met today with Jon Kilik and Preston Holmes to go over the revised nonunion budget. It came in under $5.5 million. Now Arthur Klein needs a copy so he can forward it to Universal. Yo, it's getting close. We begin preproduction four weeks from tomorrow. THAT'S THE TRUTH, RUTH.

Buggin' Out should wear an ear cuff.

I saw *Powaqqatsi* last night at the Ziegfeld. It's better than *Koyaanisqatsi*. The film is about the third world and people of color. They had this vicious shot of kids racing straight into the camera. Nasty. We should do the same.

MAY 4, 1988

Flags will be a big visual motif in *Do The Right Thing*. The red, white, and blue Puerto Rican flag; the red, white, and green Italian flag; and the red, black, and green African-American flag. Cops will wear American flags on their uniforms.

The fire hydrant-johnny pump should be painted fire-truck red.

MAY 10, 1988

I had a great meeting with Danny Aiello yesterday at Columbus Restaurant. Danny and I had met only once before at the premiere party for Madonna's film *Who's That Girl*. We hit it off right away. Danny had me dying. Next to Blacks, Italians curse the best. Danny likes the script and wants to do the project.

Yesterday Giancarlo called from Detroit. He wanted to know the deal about Fishburne. I told him what Larry told me about only accepting leading roles now. I told Giancarlo he'd have to talk to Fish because I can't worry about it.

The same goes for Matt Dillon, he's jerking me around. I mentioned this to Danny who said Matt is always like that. It might be his manager, Vic Ramos. Regardless, I might go with John Turturro, that motherfucker can act his ass off.

Turturro lives in Brooklyn, Park Slope. Today I got him to tape *Five Corners* for me. His work in that film is frightening. Turturro, Roger Smith, and Rock Dutton went to the School of Drama at Yale while my brother was an undergraduate there.

We wanna go into preproduction on May 31 and so far no paper is signed. What the fuck is going on? I gotta get on Arthur Klein.

MAY 12, 1988

I've made two major decisions today. Larry Fishburne and Matt Dillon are out. Larry never had a leading role before *School Daze*. If he wants to wait another fifteen years, I wish him luck. I gotta make my film. I'm rolling with Bill Nunn for Radio Raheem. He'll be great.

Tomorrow night I'm going to the Yankee game with Danny Aiello. I hope he'll do the film. It's funny, Danny Aiello, Richard Edson, and John Turturro all look similar. They could be family. It's scary.

This afternoon Ruby Dee and Ossie Davis are coming by the office. They want to talk to me about adding depth to Da Mayor and Mother Sister. I'll be all ears and taking notes.

I M A G E

A kid pushing another kid in a shopping cart down the block.

MAY 16, 1988

I'm listening to a tape that Ruby Dee and Ossie Davis made for me. They came up with character backgrounds that I want to incorporate into the script. Da Mayor was given his title by some people a long time ago. He's the only one who still takes it seriously. He drinks but he loves Mother Sister. She despises him.

When Da Mayor recalls his past, it's gotta be a killer. He should be dogged by the young people on the block. They call him a bum, a drunk.

DA MAYOR

> Until you have stood in the doorway and heard the hungry cries of your five children, you don't know shit. You don't know the pain. Don't call me a drunk, a bum. You don't know me. The best thing I could do was leave them.

Mother Sister is too through with the community. She owns the brownstone she lives in, but has been threatening to sell it for years and move to Long Island. Her father was a wealthy West Indian who owned a business and a good amount of property. When he died it was left to his daughter. Mother Sister married a man who lost it all except the house she lives in, which is also the house she was born in.

Mother Sister tells Jade she was the princess of the block until she let that fool man talk her into marrying him.

Mother Sister saves Da Mayor from being trampled in the riot. She takes him back to her house. The next morning, Da Mayor wakes up in Mother Sister's big brass bed. Mother Sister says "Good morning, Ya Honor." When Da Mayor objects she says, "What else am I suppose to call you?"

MAY 16, 1988

At this moment, there is no film. The tops Universal will go is $6 million. We went over the budget this past Saturday. This is a $7.5 million picture. It's up to Universal. Today and tomorrow are crucial. I told Arthur Klein that we should give the script to Orion Pictures.

We sent a new, revised budget to Universal, they have to let us know something soon. They have us in a sticky position.

John Turturro called me from L.A. He's out there doing a film for Dennis Hopper. He loves my script and wants to do it. There is still a question in his mind about which role would be best for him and best for the film. Right now he's leaning towards Pino. He's right.

I've been listening to "Cool Jerk" by the Capitols. It's a real classic, fast and upbeat, and it brings to mind summer in the city. This may be the song for the opening credits sequence. I see Rosie Perez dancing to "Cool Jerk" all over Brooklyn at the first heat of dawn. Rosie doing the Cool Jerk on the Brooklyn Bridge, on the promenade, and on various rooftops.

Jade should have a one-bedroom apartment. When we first meet Mookie, we see him sleeping on his sister's sofa. Also, I have to rethink Buggin' Out. He's too political to be a b-boy and I don't want to change that.

Sam Kitt suggested a montage scene where Buggin' Out is trying to recruit people to boycott Sal's Famous Pizzeria. It would be a quick-cutting montage. Everyone Buggin' Out asks says no, except for Radio Raheem.

I have an idea. When I see the young brothers and sisters out in the street, they can't stand still, they're always moving and dancing. Music isn't necessarily playing, maybe it's just in their heads. I'll have Mookie, Buggin' Out, and Radio Raheem dancing in place, even in certain dialogue scenes.

It's Saturday afternoon and we're waiting word from Universal Pictures on the final budget. We're set to start preproduction a week from Tuesday. They gotta tell us something.

MAY 23, 1988

Universal Pictures is dicking me around. They won't budge from the $6.5 million budget, won't go a penny over it. It's ridiculous. White boys get real money, fuck up, lose millions of dollars, and still get chance after chance. Not so with us. You fuck up one time, that's it. After the commercial successes of *She's Gotta Have It* and *School Daze,* I shouldn't have to fight for the pennies the way I'm doing now. But what else can I do? I'll make the best film possible with the budget I'm given.

MAY 25, 1988

We finally settled on $6.5 million with Universal. Because of the budget crunch, we'll have to shoot this film in eight weeks instead of nine. We're also going with a union crew, which takes a big chunk of our budget. Wynn Thomas has started to design the sets. We start construction this Tuesday.

This Tuesday marks seven weeks until we shoot. I've got to cut down on my other shit. Right now we're cutting three commercials for Nike featuring Charles Barkley.

MAY 29, 1988

It's 11:00 A.M. Sunday morning. I only slept a couple of hours last night. We had another Forty Acres and a Mule Sneaker Jam at the Puck Building. As usual, it was one of the all-time great parties.

Robi Reed and Ruthe Carter came to town for the party. I met with them both to discuss the casting and costuming work that lies ahead for us during preproduction.

We're gonna have the tightest crew on this film. It's gonna be too tight. As Randy Fletcher, the assistant director, said last night, it's gonna be tight as chicken pussy, and that's tight.

Tomorrow *School Daze* opens in Toronto. I'll spend the day there promoting the film but my biggest priority now is to finish this second draft of *Do The Right Thing.*

It is the time to become super-focused. Tuesday we finish the commercials featuring Charles Barkley for Nike and that's it. We'll wait to do the Air Jordan spot until after we finish shooting the film. It's bad enough I have to go to London for a couple of days to promote *School Daze,* two weeks before we start to shoot *Do The Right Thing.*

Yesterday I came up with the idea for a *Do The Right Thing* T-shirt. It has flags on the front, and on the back, the tag line:

THIS IS AMERICA
(it's no comedy)

JUNE 3, 1988

Last night I went to see Brother Minister Farrakhan at Friendship Baptist Church. He gave a rousing speech and made positive remarks about my work.

We starting shooting six weeks from Monday. As of this weekend, no, as of today, I'm on a mission. I'm gonna concentrate 100 percent on the script. That's my job right now. Fuck the bullshit.

Wynn Thomas came up with a great idea, to turn one of the abandoned buildings on the block into a storefront church:

THE YES-JESUS LAST BAPTIST CHURCH

JUNE 7, 1988

I'm writing like a madman to finish the second draft of *Do The Right Thing.* I have to go out to L.A. next Thursday to meet with the head honchos at Universal. I'll implore them to promote the film properly and spend the money that needs to be spent.

Danny Aiello's mother died Saturday night. We were supposed to meet at Columbus Restaurant, but he couldn't leave his mom's bedside. Danny sent his two sons instead, Danny Jr. and Rick. One's a stuntman, the other's a boxer/actor.

JUNE 8, 1988

I've been rewriting the script for the last three or four days, and I finally finished the second draft. I'll have it retyped this afternoon.

Robi Reed is scheduled to read Rosie Perez in L.A. before she comes to New York this weekend to begin casting. I wrote a monologue for Rosie and had it Faxed to Robi. I have complete confidence in Rosie. She's gonna be a great discovery.

Beginning the film with Rosie dancing to "Cool Jerk" is gonna be nasty. Ernest suggested that we shoot Rosie dancing in front of backdrops of various locations in Brooklyn. We'll use a rear-screen projector to create this effect.

JUNE 10, 1988

The second draft of *Do The Right Thing* came in at ninety-two-and-one-eighth pages. Lean and mean. If we have a 39-day shooting schedule, we can average 2.3 pages a day, which is nothing. If the weather cooperates, the shoot should be fast and smooth.

Universal Pictures finally wired us $150,000 in start-up money. We had to scratch to get that. I've had to put up a substantial amount of my own money already.

Last night Robi Reed read Rosie Perez in L.A. I called Robi this morning. She said that Rosie went crazy. She tore it up. She knew exactly who Tina Rampolla is. I'm glad; I wanted Rosie to get the role. I called Rosie immediately, woke her up, and told her she had the part. She couldn't believe it, and went back to sleep.

The songwriter Raymond Jones sent me the rough idea of the cut Radio Raheem will play on his box throughout the film. I've been waiting at least a month for the song. I like the basic idea, but it needs work. I brought a copy over to Bill Stepney at Def Jam. I called him later in the day and he wasn't too enthusiastic. He's gonna give it to Hank Shockney to play around with. I'll also send the cassette to Chuck D. of Public Enemy. He's gonna write lyrics for it.

We're gonna ask Raymond Jones to do the station jingles for We Love Radio, 108 on your FM dial.

I think this obsession that Black youth has with gold is nuts. Their value system is out of whack. I don't want to pump up gold by flaunting it in this film. Instead I'll have actors wear African-influenced jewelry and accessories. That's the real deal.

Everyone working on the film must remember that it takes place a year from now. This must be first and foremost in people's minds. We have to anticipate what folks will be wearing next summer.

I want actors and extras to wear bicycle pants and cutoff sweatpants. Mookie should wear a big bowling shirt embroidered with "Sal's Famous Pizzeria."

In the summertime Black folks always put baby powder on themselves. You see folks walking around with white necks. We should have a scene where a bottle of Johnson & Johnson Baby Powder is being passed around.

JUNE 13, 1988

Now that the second draft is done and most of the principal casting is complete, I can start planning the shots for the film. Time is slipping by. When I get back from London, there will be exactly one week left before we shoot. That's no time at all. Tomorrow Ernest and I are gonna spend some time together talking over the script, thinking about shots, lighting, and camera moves.

We should have a group of kids from a day care center walk through a shot holding hands.

The final shot of the film should be similar to that stylized shot in *Hair* where everyone comes out at once onto an empty street. As Mookie walks away from Sal's, the empty street comes to life.

Robi Reed and her assistant, her sister Andrea, arrived in New York today. Things are really jumping off at the office. We shoot five weeks from today. It's right around the corner, no time at all.

This Thursday afternoon Monty and I are flying out to Los Angeles. We're having dinner with Sean Daniels, Jim Jacks, and Sam Kitt, the honchos at Universal. Then Friday we're set to meet the studio's marketing, advertising, and publicity departments. Monty and I have to fire them up, so they'll sell this film properly and insure that it is seen. What happened with *School Daze* and Columbia Pictures cannot happen again.

Today John Kilik, Ernest, and I went over to the set. I was fired up. It's amazing how fast the construction is proceeding. We're actually making a movie, and it's gonna be a motherfucker!

JUNE 16, 1988

Monty and I are on the MGM Grand First Class flight to Los Angeles to meet with the suits, the executives at Universal.

Our meeting with the marketing, advertising, and publicity departments is crucial. The people at Universal don't know me personally. They've heard the rumor that Spike Lee is a wild-eyed Black militant, a baby Malcolm X. I bet they've also heard that I'm difficult to work with, which is not the case at all.

Any Black man who is intelligent, opinionated, and who doesn't smile ha-ha, chee-chee continuously, is immediately branded as difficult. I'm not difficult, I just know exactly what I want. I happen to have a different agenda than some filmmakers. Studios don't give a flying fuck about hiring Black people but I do. The little power I have I'm gonna use to put qualified people Black people on my team. What good is power or influence if it can't be put to good use? And by good use I don't mean getting a motherfucking table at Spago's. Motherfuck, Spago's! If I can get some people jobs, then that's the truth, Ruth!

What I hope to do at this meeting is forge a partnership. That's what I had with Columbia until David Puttnam got the boot. We want to alleviate Universal's anxieties about this person Spike Lee. I might start off like this: "If you don't believe those stories about Spike Lee, I won't believe those stories about Universal. The Black Tower."

I've been back from L.A. two days. We shoot in less than four weeks. Today we had our first full production meeting. It went quite well. Time, my time especially, is getting squished.

This weekend Roger Smith, who played one of the Gammites in *School Daze,* talked his way into *Do The Right Thing.* He has been bugging me from Day One.

In the first draft of the script I had a character named Smiley. I cut him out in the second draft. Now I'm putting him back in. The kids call him Smiley cause he never smiles. I told Roger Smith I wanted Smiley to be retarded. Roger came up with the idea that Smiley should stutter, listen to Malcolm's speeches on a Walkman, and give out cards with that famous photograph of Malcolm X and Martin. Apparently, it's the only photograph of them together.

When Buggin' Out is trying to recruit people to boycott Sal's, the only people he enlists are Radio Raheem and Smiley. When Sal's is burning, Smiley goes back into the flaming pizzeria and puts the photo of Malcolm X and Martin up on the Wall of Fame. For the first time in the film, he smiles. It's a great suggestion of Roger's. I have to give it to him.

I'm sick as a dog with a sinus cold and still sore from playing softball the other day. Feeling under the weather made me grumpy. I can be that way sometimes.

The days are getting hotter and muggier. I have to make better use of my time. We shoot in less than four weeks. I have to finish going over the shots for the film and learn my lines.

Casting has been coming along well. There are still some key spots open. Joe Seneca can't do the role of ML. He has a picture where he can make a substantial amount of money. This is understandable. To replace Joe Seneca, we're thinking about Bill Cobb, James Earl Jones, or Paul Benjamin.

Up for grabs are the roles of the yuppie Clifton, officers Ponte and Long, and Charlie, the guy whose car gets drenched. The kids, Ahmad, Cee, Punchy, and Ella are also up for grabs. We're leaning towards unknowns for those roles. We're considering Wesley Snipes, Leonard Thomas, and this new guy Martin Lawrence. I'll see all these people next week. Robi begins callbacks next week as well.

Ruby Dee and Ossie Davis want more money, they deserve it. I wish the budget allowed for it. I hope they'll agree to our offer. We just found out that Ruby Dee is doing the play *Checkmates* on Broadway. The only days she'll be able to shoot beyond 5:00 P.M. are Mondays.

Danny Aiello is fine. He's more gung-ho than anyone.

We've secured the photos of Italian-American entertainers and athletes for the Wall of Fame and the photo of Malcolm X and Martin. Again, I must say, using that photo was a stroke of genius on Roger Smith's part. We also hooked up the Louisville Slugger Mickey Mantle bats for Sal to have behind the pizza counter. What about the Mister Softee Truck!! Who's working on it?

DIALOGUE

You need to quit.

JUNE 23, 1988

Today I have a meeting with Charles Milne, chairman of the film department at New York University. Something has to be done to get more Black students into the film school. The school must start recruiting aggressively. None of this wait-and-see-if-Blacks-apply shit. That's not gonna get it. Ads should be taken out in *Jet, Ebony, Essence,* and *Black Collegian*.

I have to speak to an auditorium full of junior high school students in Bed-Stuy. Their school board is allowing us to use their building as a holding area for the cast during the entire shoot.

JUNE 26, 1988

Tomorrow we begin the serious countdown. It's three weeks till we commence principal photography. Yesterday was productive. Ruthe Carter and I went shopping for the principal actors' costumes. Robi and I started to audition actors for supporting roles. We made a bunch of casting choices. I still have to decide on the kids, Ahmad, Punchy, Ella, and Cee. This film has to be cast before I leave for London to open *School Daze.*

JUNE 29, 1988

It's funny. The more films I do, the less it's about the film and the more it is about the deal. I agree that agents are necessary, but they're still one of the lowest forms of life. It's a drag dealing with them. That's why I try to establish a rapport with an actor first. Then I go to the agent. I know it must piss the agent off, because my good relationship with the actor makes his job less important. The actor may start feeling too independent. He may begin to think he can generate his own work. Then the agent might lose his 10 percent. Everyone wants to make some money, I'm not complaining about that. But actors and agents must realize that landing a role in one of my films does not mean big money. Not yet, at least. So far I have had budgets of $175,000, $5.8 million, and $6.5 million. That isn't a lot of money by industry standards. The average budget for a Hollywood feature in 1987 was $18 million.

Actors should reprimand their agents for some of the bold liberties they take. They refuse offers and blow deals without even consulting the actors.

Case in point is Tisha Campbell, or better yet, her mother/manager, Mona Campbell. Under the instruction of her mother, Tisha sued me last week. Her suit involves two songs on the *School Daze* songtrack album. One is "Be Alone Tonight," written by Raymond Jones. This song is sung by The Rays, Tisha, Jasmine Guy, Paula Brown, and Angela Ali.

From the beginning I saw "Be Alone Tonight" as a girl group number. It was never intended to be a Tisha Campbell vehicle. The royalties were to be split evenly between the singers. Mona wanted Tisha to receive a disproportionate amount of the royalties. She also insisted that Tisha be credited as lead singer. What's worse is on "Straight and Nappy," *School Daze's* big production number, where Tisha is one of twenty-four singers, Mona wants her daughter to receive one-fourth of these royalties.

We've tried to negotiate with Mona, but she refused to accept anything offered. We couldn't hold up the soundtrack album, so it was released without Tisha's signed contract. On advisement from my lawyer, I settled out of court. I gave Tisha $25,000 of my motherfucking, hard-earned money.

Tisha Campbell is one of the most gifted and talented young actresses out there today. She's a major talent, but her moms/manager is another story. Mona will become a hindrance to Tisha's career, because people don't want to deal with her.

I wish Tisha all the best. She's a trouper. But one day—mark my words—Tisha is gonna have to make the painful decision to cut her moms loose as her manager.

JUNE 30, 1988

It's 7:30 A.M. and I'm up. We shoot two weeks from this Monday. This weekend is the Independence Day holiday, but my butt is gonna be right here working around the clock. Ernest and I have been going over the shots, but there's still more work to be done in that regard. It's funny, two weeks before you shoot, there are eight million things to do. It always happens.

JULY 4, 1988

The character Smiley needs work. He will be in the background throughout the entire film. He is constantly ridiculed and laughed at. Some ideas:

1. Smiley is made fun of by Ahmad, Cee, Punchy, and Ella.

2. Smiley comes into Sal's Famous Pizzeria.

3. Smiley is recruited by Buggin' Out and Radio Raheem to boycott Sal's.

4. When static starts in the pizzeria between Sal and the boycott crew, Smiley is frightened. He ducks into a corner with his hands pressed over his ears trying to block out the noise of the fight.

5. Sal's Famous Pizzeria is burning. Smiley goes to the Wall of Fame and puts up the photo of Malcolm and Martin.

JULY 7, 1988

Monty and I are in London doing publicity for the opening of *School Daze*. We are keeping in constant contact with the office in Brooklyn, sending Faxes back and forth. Everything is coming along fine, but soon I'm gonna have to start learning my lines. Spike, ya gotta know your lines!

G R A F I T T I

CRAZY EDDIE MUST GO
TAWANA DIDN'T LIE
TAWANA TOLD THE TRUTH
DUMP KOCH

JULY 9, 1988

Monty and I are on our way back to Nueva York. It's been a fun-filled, hard-working four days in London. It's gonna take this entire weekend to turn my body clock around. We start shooting a week from Monday, we're talking eight days. Eight days!

THINGS TO DO WHEN I GET BACK

1. Go to dentist to be fitted for Mookie's gold tooth.

2. Meet with Sam Mattingly, our unit publicist.

3. Check with the property master about the Malcolm/Martin cards.

4. Videotape Sam Jackson (Mister Señor Love Daddy).

5. Videotape Rosie Perez (Tina).

6. Check with Raymond Jones about the station jingles for We Love radio. They should be humorous. Tell Raymond that Public Enemy will write Radio Raheem's theme song, but he should hold on to his demo.

7. Vito should wear a sleeveless white T-shirt.

8. We need *Do The Right Thing* T-shirts for the actors.

9. Videotape the Corner Men—Paul Benjamin, Robin Harris, and Frankie Faison.

10. Check with Wynn to see if he's gotten the locations needed for the Hot, Hotter, Hottest Montage.

11. Call Nike to get new sneakers for Mookie.

12. We should use the double dutch girls as background in Scene 52.

13. Spike, it's time to write the montage scene where Buggin' Out tries to recruit people to boycott Sal's.

14. What's the deal with the copyright on the Mister Softee tune? Can we use it?

15. Call Coke. Are they down for product placement or what? (Coke is shaky.)

16. Call Arthur Klein's office to see if they've found out about the rights to the song "Cool Jerk" yet.

17. In Scene 93, the voices of the mob should be given to specific characters.

18. For the final scene, some of the extras should be in their Sunday best on their way to the storefront church, the Yes Jesus Last

Baptist Church. I should make a note for the score. The music might be kind of churchy here.

July 11—Meeting with Eddie Smith, the stunt coordinator.
July 12—Full production meeting, 7:00 A.M.
        Read-through with full cast, 9:00 A.M.
        Set rehearsal schedule for actors.
        Do breakdown of when principals will be needed as background in a given scene.

JULY 13, 1988

Today was the second day of rehearsal. I was a little tired. I have to start my vitamin pack again before we shoot Monday.

JULY 14, 1988

Two more days of rehearsal. Last night I read half of the script before I fell asleep. I woke up at five this morning to complete it.

My rehearsal schedule today:

9–11:00 A.M.	Jade, Mother Sister, Da Mayor
11–noon	Ella, Ahmad, Punchy, Cee, Da Mayor
noon–1:00 P.M.	Lunch/meeting with unit publicist
1–3:00 P.M.	Sal, Vito, Pino, Mookie, Joie
3–5:00 P.M.	Radio Raheem, Buggin Out, Mookie, Sal, Vito
5–6:00 P.M.	Tina & Mookie

JULY 16, 1988

Two days before we shoot. Yesterday was the last day of formal rehearsal. I got my gold tooth. Larry Cherry hooked up my haircut and I feel ready. I've got my game face on.

Last night Danny Aiello and I did a radio play by John Patrick Shanley for National Public Radio. It was fun. I had never done anything like that before. Afterward the three of us talked about acting. Danny said, "Spike, you're a good actor, very natural, you just have to get an activity. Your body, you have to work on it." He hit it on the nose. As an actor sometimes I do feel awkward just standing there. Danny was 100 percent right.

Mookie has to have an activity. Maybe he's always shuffling his feet. He has to do something. Another idea just came to me. Mookie might sound a little bit Italian—his intonations and the expressions he uses. He's worked at Sal's for so long, it's rubbed off.

Today we had a block party for the neighborhood, for the community of Bedford-Stuyvesant. Everybody showed up: Danny Aiello, Sean Penn, Ossie Davis, Melvin Van Peebles, Monty gave a fired-up speech. It was a historic day. We're making history, people are down with us, and it's all being documented.

My character Mookie is finally coming together. This afternoon I gave a friend $1,000 to buy me the biggest diamond earring on Canal Street. That's Mookie. I have my earring, my gold tooth, and a vicious cut from Larry Cherry. All I need is an activity, and I'm on my way.

Tonight I'm gonna work on the script. Tomorrow is gonna be totally chill. I'll relax. I might watch one or two movies on tape. That's it.

Actually, the first thing I'm gonna do tomorrow morning is write Buggin' Out's boycott montage. Finally! Then I'll go through the shot list and look over all the scenes we're scheduled to shoot the first week.

JULY 17, 1988

It's Sunday afternoon, the day before we start shooting *Do The Right Thing*. I feel good, but I'm still gonna chill out today. Be still. Yesterday I read the script three times and went over my shot list for the week. It's a strange coincidence that we begin shooting on the same day that the Democratic Convention opens in Atlanta.

(The Democrats are trying to stroke Jesse.) Ernest told me that July 18 is also Nelson Mandela's birthday.

JULY 23, 1988

It's Saturday morning after our first week of shooting. The week went well, especially for a first week. There are wrinkles that still need to be ironed out. On Monday, the first day, crowd control was a mess, but it got better as the week went on.

The weather fucked with us the first week, though. Wednesday it poured. Thursday we had to go to a cover set. Friday we started inside, but moved outside and did all the Corner Men's primary scenes. That was six pages of dialogue, which is a lot.

When you're not shooting a film, you forget how fucking hard it is. Making films has got to be one of the hardest endeavors known to humankind. I got a quick reminder of this during our first week. The first shot we did was one of the most difficult shots of the film. It's the scene where Mookie leaves his house and walks down the block greeting various people. The camera follows me for the entire stretch. It's a one-shot scene involving tricky choreography.

When you're shooting, the end is never in sight. If it is, it's a very small light at the end of a long, long, dark tunnel. Dag, I don't see how David Lean spent a year in the desert on *Lawrence of Arabia* or in the jungle on *Bridge on the River Kwai*. He wasn't a young motherfucker either. Straight up and down, film work is hard as shit.

Yesterday was Roger Smith's first day of work. His character Smiley is gonna be the hype. He walks up and down the block listening to Malcolm X's speech "The Ballot and the Bullet" on a cassette in his Walkman and selling colored-in copies of the Malcolm/Martin photo. We shot a scene on a staircase with Mookie and Smiley. I'm delivering a pizza and Smiley tries to sell me some cards. I want to add a scene to the film with Smiley and Jade—pure ad lib.

After this film, forget about it, Joie is gonna be a star. She looks beautiful on film. Stunning is the correct word. Soon I should write a leading role for her. She's that good. And I'm not saying this because she's my sister.

JULY 24, 1988

It's early Sunday morning. We need good weather all next week to stay on schedule. I spent the entire weekend resting and preparing for the week to come. There are a couple of big scenes to do. The johnny pump scene shoots Tuesday and Wednesday. It's gonna be a mother, it's five-and-a-half pages. I'm gonna go over the shot list for that now.

Tomorrow, Spike, do not forget your director's viewfinder. You have a five-dollar bet with Ernest that you won't forget it.

JULY 31, 1988

We've completed two weeks of principal photography. I flew down to Atlanta last night for the First National Black Arts Festival. The organizers plan to stage the festival one every two years. I'm gonna speak today for an hour, then there's a screening of all the work I've ever done. Damn, a retrospective already. Hold it now, I'm not dead yet!

I'm on a flight back to Nueva York now. My speech this afternoon went well. In addition to the film, they actually screened all my music videos, trailers, and commercials. My grandmother came to the event. It was good for her to hear me talk and see the work. But that's over now. We're back to the third week of shooting.

Tomorrow morning we shoot the first stunt I've ever directed. It's the scene where Da Mayor saves little Eddie from being hit by a car. I hope it doesn't turn into a drawn-out process like the fire hydrant scene. Once we hit two or three weeks straight of good weather, we'll be rolling.

I want to write a scene for Officer Ponte and Officer Long as they patrol the block. It'll be a car rig.

We've been shooting for three weeks; we're almost at the halfway point.

I'm learning so much more with each film. It's been said that directing films is like being a psychologist. It's so true. Actors are quirky people. I'm learning to deal with them. Larry Fishburne's big complaint on *School Daze* was I didn't communicate enough. I've taken this to heart on *Do The Right Thing*.

I've come to see that my style of directing is about a controlled freedom, if there is such a thing. I give actors an enormous amount of freedom to shape their characters. I try to give them the framework or boundaries to work in. For some actors, this presents a problem. In the past they've been restricted and held back. When they are given the ball and told to run with it, they don't know what to do.

When this film is released people are gonna make a big deal out of the fact that this is my first film to use white actors. I know I'm gonna hear the question again and again, "Spike, is there a difference between directing Black actors and white actors?" and I'll answer, "Sir, I think that's a stupid-ass question."

I have yet to read an interview in which Woody Allen has been asked why he doesn't use Black people in his films. But I'm interrogated all the time about not using white actors. And now that I've used white actors, people are gonna want to know what the big difference is. There is none.

One of the treasures of shooting this film so far is being in the presence of Ossie Davis. He's a giant—forty-two years in the arts. He's known everybody from Zora Neale Hurston to Malcolm X. I just sit back and listen to him. It's also interesting seeing him and Ruby together. They have me dying. I've never seen two people in love like that before. I'm sure they have their share of arguments, all couples do. But being married all this time, working together, and still in love, whew! If I could have a marriage like that. I gotta talk to them and get the secret. There probably isn't any secret, just a lot of hard work.

It's a great pleasure to make this film in Brooklyn, in Bedford-Stuyvesant. Y'know Spike, you're lucky. I'm young, Black, and doing what I want to do. That's why I say my prayers every night. I'm doing what makes me the happiest, that's making films.

I've said this so often before, but why not again? Ninety-five per-cent of the people on this planet work all their lives, get up every morning, and drag themselves to a job they hate, a job they really despise. They end up going to the grave that way. It's sad, but true. I'm one of the lucky ones, but that doesn't mean I go around singing "Don't Worry Be Happy." Sometimes on the set, while we're setting up for a shot, I look around and watch everyone working. I see all these young, talented Black artists and technicians and I feel just fine. It's a good feeling to be in a position to hire people who need jobs, people who deserve jobs. Of course we can't hire everyone, but we're doing what we can.

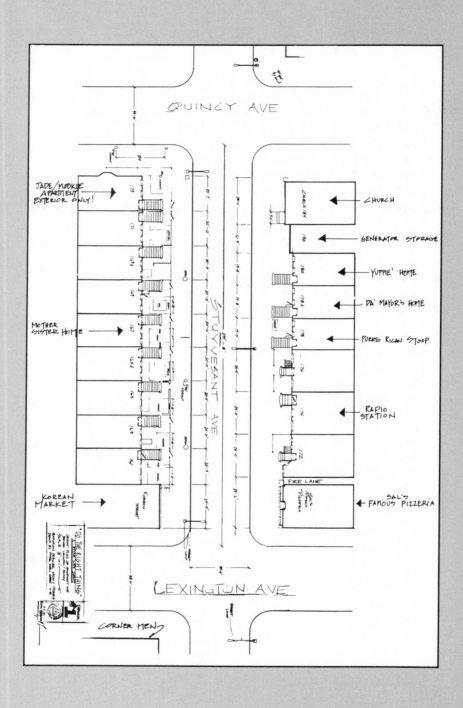

QUINCY AVE

JADE/MOOKIE
APARTMENT
EXTERIOR ONLY! →

CHURCH ←

GENERATOR STORAGE ←

YUPPIE' HOME ←

DA' MAYOR'S HOME ←

MOTHER
SISTER HOME →

PUERTO RICAN STOOP ←

RADIO
STATION ←

STUYVESANT AVE.

FIRE LANE

KOREAN
MARKET →

SAL'S
FAMOUS PIZZERIA ←

"DO THE RIGHT THING"

LEXINGTON AVE

CORNER MEN

PART II.

PRODUCTION

NOTES

Do *The Right Thing* was my first union film. To keep our costs down, Universal suggested that we shoot the film with a nonunion crew someplace outside of New York, like Philadelphia or Baltimore. I'm sorry, Philly and Baltimore are great cities, but they just aren't Brooklyn. This film had to be shot in Brooklyn, if it was to be done all. However, there was no way we could shoot a $6.5 million film in New York city without giving the film unions a piece of the action.

On every film, I try to use as many Black people behind the camera as possible. A major concern I had about shooting with an all-union crew was whether this would prevent me from hiring as many Blacks as I wanted. There are few minorities in the film unions, and, historically, film unions have done little to encourage Blacks and women to join their ranks.

Originally we planned to sign a contract with the International Alliance of Theatrical State Employees (IATSE, or IA) because they have more Black members. They proved to be too expensive, so we entered into negotiations with the National Association of Broadcast Employees and Technicians (NABET). The negotiations with NABET lasted a month, but we were able to win some important concessions.

One concession was that NABET allowed us to hire a number of Blacks to work on the film who were not members of the union, including Larry Cherry, our hairstylist, my brother David Lee, the still photographer, and Darnell Martin, the second assistant cameraperson. (At the time, there were no Blacks in these union categories.) In addition, we were able to hire some nonunion people as trainees in the grip and electric departments. NABET agreed to consider granting union membership to these people if their work on the film proved satisfactory. Eventually they were admitted to the union.

We cut a similar deal with the Teamsters union, which is responsible for all the vehicles driven on a union shoot. The Teamsters have the right to determine how many drivers are assigned to a union production. At $1,500 to $2,000 per week per driver, this can eat a hole in your budget. The Teamsters allowed us to hire a small number of union drivers and use nonunion production assistants to supplement this group. Out of the five union drivers they assigned to the production, two were Black.

I wanted to film *Do The Right Thing* entirely on one block. Our location scout combed the streets of Brooklyn for two weeks and came back with a book of photos. One Saturday, Wynn Thomas, the production designer, and I visited all the locations suggested by our scout. It turned out the block that we chose was the first one he had looked at—Stuyvesant Street between Lexington and Quincy avenues, in the heart of the Bedford-Stuyvesant section of Brooklyn.

The block had everything that we needed: brownstones which weren't too upscale or too dilapidated. And, most importantly, it had two empty lots that faced each other, where we could build sets for the Korean market and Sal's Famous Pizzeria. Once we decided on the block, Wynn went to work designing the sets and supervising construction.

I think it was Monty Ross's idea to hire the Fruit of Islam, the security force of the Nation of Islam, the Black Muslim organization, to patrol the set. Cops really have no respect in Black communities in New York, especially not in Bed-Stuy, where cops have been convicted in the past on drug trafficking charges. We knew we couldn't bring in a white security force, it had to be Black. And Black people who were respected in the community. All this led us to the Fruit of Islam.

It was obvious that crack was being sold on the block. One of the first things we did was let the crack dealers know they weren't welcome. We boarded up an abandoned building that was being used as a crack house and turned another into a location site. We managed to move the dealers off the block, but we weren't able to put them out of business. They just closed up shop and moved around the corner.

During preproduction, Universal asked me to recommend a filmmaker to do the electronic press kit that the studio would use to promote the film. I recommended the veteran documentary filmmaker St. Clair Bourne. When I met with St. Clair to discuss the press kit, I asked him to consider directing a film about the making of *Do The Right Thing*. We were shooting in Bed-Stuy. We were taking over an entire city block for eight weeks. And we had hired

the Fruit of Islam—Farrakhan's private security force—to patrol
the set and to close two crack houses. Certainly, this needed to be
documented. St. Clair got to work on the project immediately.

Casting for *Do The Right Thing* was on a much smaller scale
than *School Daze*. Most of the major roles I had decided upon even
before I completed the script. We held auditions in New York only,
whereas for *School Daze,* we saw actors in Los Angeles, Atlanta,
and New York. I wanted to cast white actors who feel comfortable
around Black people. A white actor nervous about setting foot in
Bed-Stuy wasn't gonna work for this film. The fact that Danny
Aiello grew up in the South Bronx, and John Turturro in a Black
neighborhood in Queens, made them ideal choices.

The first day of rehearsal the full cast met to read through the
script, then I opened up the floor for discussion and suggestions.
Paul Benjamin, who plays ML, one of the Corner Men, is a veteran
actor who I've wanted to work with for a long time. Paul was the
first actor to raise a question about script. He was worried that it
showed nothing but lazy, shiftless Black people. It seemed to Paul
that no one in the film had a job, and that his character and the
other Corner Men just hung out all day.

It was Rosie Perez (Tina), who had never acted before in her life,
who answered Paul's question. Rosie grew up in Bed-Stuy and
stayed with relatives there during the shoot. She went off on a ten-
minute tirade about how people like the Corner Men actually exist
and that Paul and everyone else should go to Bed-Stuy and take a
look.

I told Paul that *Do The Right Thing* was not about Black people
in three-piece suits going to work, it was about Black underclass in
Bed-Stuy, a community that has some of the highest unemploy-
ment, infant mortality, and drug-related homicide rates in New
York City. We're talking about people who live in the bowels of the
social-economic system, but still live with dignity and humor. Paul
and I talked about it the next day and he understood.

We spent the rest of the rehearsal week meeting in small groups
to talk about characters. When the Corner Men met for their group
rehearsal, they were having trouble getting their characters to
mesh. I decided that we should take a trip to the location and read

the dialogue there. We drove out to Stuyvesant Street and set up some chairs in the same spot where the Corner Men's scenes would be shot. Being on the set, in the community, made all the difference.

The fact this film takes on one single day was a challenge for everyone involved. Continuity was a motherfucker. Especially for Ernest, who had to make two months worth of footage to look like it was shot on one day. For the most part, he had to rely on available light, since we spent most of our time outdoors.

Though this film is about young Black people in Brooklyn, Ruthe Carter, the costume designer, and I wanted to downplay the gold fad. Besides the gold teeth that Mookie and Buggin' Out wear, and Radio Raheem's knuckle rings (which are really brass), you don't see much gold in this film. I think it's crazy for young Black kids to spend money they don't have on gold jewelry. The kids pick it up from the rappers. I mean no disrespect to L.L. Cool J and Eric B. & Rakim, but this gold-chains-by-the-ton shit is ridiculous.

I knew I wanted my character Mookie to wear tight bicycle shorts underneath a pair of loose-fitting shorts. I got this from basketball players. Instead of wearing jock straps now, many are wearing bicycle pants beneath their uniforms. I like the look because of the contrast. So I had an idea for the bottom of my costume, but I was stumped on what to wear on top.

Cecil Holmes, one of the bigwigs in Black music at CBS Records, knows I'm a baseball fan and once gave me a Jackie Robinson jersey. The night before we started shooting, I was still undecided about my costume, then I remembered the jersey.

The jersey was a good choice. I don't think Jackie Robinson has gotten his due from Black people. There are young people today, even Black athletes, who don't know what Jackie Robinson did. They might know he was the first Black Major Leaguer, but they don't know what he had to bear to make it easier for those who came after him.

When you're directing a film, it takes over your life completely. You get up at the crack of dawn, shoot for twelve to fourteen hours (if you're lucky), watch dailies, grab something to eat before you go to bed, then you're up again at the crack of dawn.

The first week of production went well. I felt we could have been better organized in terms of communication between the assistant directors and other departments, but by the end of the week it all came together.

It rained on and off for three of the days of the first week, and we were forced to shoot an interior scene, one of our precious few cover sets. There was concern about using up our cover sets so early in the shoot, since we had less than five to last us the entire shoot. But there was nothing we could do about that except pray for good weather. Depending on the size of the scene, overcast days were potential problems for us as well. Creating the effect of sunshine on a cloudy day over an area the size of a city block was something our budget didn't allow for.

We had a budget for extras on *Do The Right Thing*, which was a first for me. With no money to pay extras on *School Daze,* we could never predict if we'd get the number needed for a given scene. But if you look at the film, I think we did a good job disguising how few extras we actually had.

We had two opens calls for extras, one for members of the Screen Actors Guild, and one for nonunion actors. We also held a community open call at a church near the location, Antioch Baptist, which graciously served as our meal hall during the shoot.

We cast a core group of extras to play block residents and they worked the entire shoot. Additional extras were brought on for the big scenes. The first week of shooting we had a time coming up with a system of documenting the extras and background action scene by scene. We had to establish which core extras would be placed on various sides of the block, how long they would remain there, and how many new extras we should see in each scene. I didn't want to look at this film a year later and see the same two extras crossing through every shot. Again, this was a task made complicated by the fact that the film takes place in a 24-hour period, but was shot out of sequence.

One sequence that took forever to shoot was the johnny pump sequence, where Charlie (played by Frank Vincent) and his white convertible get drenched by the kids. We allotted two days to shoot it, but we should have been more generous because it ended up taking five.

The car had to be specially rigged to withstand all the water, and dried off between takes. And each time Frank got wet, he needed a wardrobe change. We used two cameras to film the kids playing in the hydrant. One was encased in underwater housing, and we used that camera to shoot the closeups of the hydrant. The camera department had a lot fun with it. It was orange and looked like an old diver's mask.

It's a compliment to Wynn Thomas's design work that people off the street were constantly wandering into Sal's Famous Pizzeria and the Korean Market, unaware they were sets. We spent almost a straight week shooting inside Sal's Famous Pizzeria. With the heat from the lights, and the crew and actors packed into one room, it really got hot in there. As soon as a take was over, people rushed to turn on the air conditioner. During lunch break, crew members used the booths as beds and caught some shut-eye.

Despite the heat, we were able to get through these interior scenes pretty quickly. John Turturro exploded one day over the prop pizza. The property master didn't have enough pies on set for John and Richard Edson to actually cut them into slices. They were told to fake it. John went off. He refused to fake it because it suspended all his belief in the scene. He was right. We saw dailies the next night and had to reshoot all the fake cutting.

I was pleased with the way we staged the conversation about "niggers" vs. "Blacks" that Mookie and Pino have in the pizzeria. As it reads in the script, the scene could have been a yelling match. It works just as well as a simple conversation, and it manages to keep the same intensity. There is enough yelling and screaming in this movie as it is.

Pino and Mookie's scene sets up the racial-slur sequence. Jump-cut sequences featuring a group of characters speaking toward the camera have been a staple of each of my films so far. *She's Gotta Have It* has the Dogs, *School Daze* has Half-Pint's unsuccessful attempt to pick up girls, and *Do The Right Thing* has representatives of different ethnic groups slurring each other.

In the first two films, the camera remains static while the subjects talk. I wanted to vary this formula a bit in *Do The Right Thing,* so I had the camera move in quickly to the person speaking. It was Ernest's idea to have the final actor in the sequence, Mister Señor

Love Daddy, come toward camera. We hooked up Love Daddy's chair to a trick wire so it looks like he's being propelled by magic.

The racial-slur sequence was meant to rouse emotions. It's funny the way people react to it. They laugh at every slur except the one directed at their ethnic group. While we were watching the dailies of Pino's slur of Blacks, a woman in the Kraft Services department started hissing at John. She couldn't separate John from his character and was less than courteous to him for the rest of the shoot.

Some of the best acting in the film happens in the scene where Pino asks his father to sell the pizzeria. Danny, John, and I tinkered with the dialogue while the crew was setting up for the shot. We finally got it down, but we still didn't have a clincher to end the scene. I was always on the lookout for ways to work Smiley into the film, since for the most part, he wasn't scripted. It hit me that we could end the scene by having Smiley knock on the pizzeria window and interrupt Danny and John's conversation.

Danny and John are sitting at a table in front of the pizzeria window. What makes that scene so great to me is that as Danny tells John about the neighborhood and why he has chosen to remain there, through the window you can see activity on the block. It lends visual support to Danny's speech.

Even if principal actors didn't have dialogue in a scene, we often used them in the background, walking down the street or hanging out, to give a sense that their characters really lived on the block. Most of the deals we made with our principals were for eight weeks of work—the entire shoot—so we could have them on standby for that very reason.

The climactic fight in the pizzeria was just as I envisioned it—a messy street fight, complete with choking and biting. It starts inside the pizzeria and ends up outside on the pavement. After Sal demolishes Radio Raheem's box with his baseball bat, we wanted to do a shot where Raheem would grab Sal by the neck, slam his face into the counter, and drag him the length of the counter.

Danny refused to do the shot. He felt it was slapstick and had been done a million times. Some cast members felt that Danny's refusal was a question of ego, of not wanting to be wasted that bad on screen. I sat down with Eddie Smith, the stunt coordinator, Danny, Danny Jr., Aiello's son and stunt double, and Bill Nunn, to hear the opinions of all involved. I decided that Bill should pull Danny over the counter instead of giving him a "facial." Danny was still not totally satisfied, but we proceeded anyway.

The cast was spurred on by Danny's reluctance to cooperate with what we had planned for the fight scene. As if to compensate for Danny's lapse of team spirit, they worked extra hard to make the scene realistic. Everyone suffered their share of bruises, including Martin Lawrence (Cee) who took a nasty shot in the eye.

Good things come out of adversity. I think the compromise we came up with made for a better shot, and I'm grateful to Danny for standing his ground. There was no tension on my part because of our disagreement. I think Danny felt isolated from the cast for a while. But I noticed that in no time he was back to his usual habit of hugging on everyone. Conflicts are bound to crop up on a film shoot. There are always differences of interpretation.

The riot scene was more involved than anything I've done on film before. Just the sheer numbers of people and vehicles involved—from extras to special-effects coordinators, from cop cars and paddy wagons to fire trucks—made it a big deal.

In order to capture all the action in the scene, we had to burn the pizzeria in stages, starting with the interior and moving outside. A big concern was how many days the pizzeria would hold up under the fire. If the fire got out of hand or the set caved in before we finished shooting the riot, we'd be up shit's creek with no paddle. But things worked out and we were able to get all the shots we wanted without losing the pizzeria.

My most pressured moment as an actor on this film was definitely when I had to throw the garbage can through the pizzeria window. No one thought about this beforehand, but the window glass was almost one-quarter inch thick. Breaking glass that thick is no easy feat. I was throwing hard, but it took four or five takes before I could get the garbage can through the window. On one take it even bounced off like a rubber ball. I was on the spot: We were filming with a special crane that had to be sent back to the rental house the next day, and the sun was coming up. Finally we got the shot.

The first night we shot the firemen turning their hoses on the crowd, the water pressure wasn't forceful enough. The stuntmen were overacting to compensate for it. The whole effect was fake, so we redid the shot the following evening.

The script called for a number of stunts involving characters getting swept away by the force of the water. Ruby Dee and my sister Joie were to get hit by a blast of water and go flying down the street. I decided the scene was powerful enough without these stunts. I cut them and came up with a different way to end the scene. Ruby Dee is in the middle of the street screaming hysterically because of all the chaos around her. Da Mayor comforts her with a hug.

Sam Jackson pointed out to me that he had the honor of acting in the first scene we shot of *School Daze* (he played one of the local yokels), and in the last scene we shot of *Do The Right Thing* (Mister Señor Love Daddy wakes up the Block). I hope this means luck for both of us.

Most wrap days are joyous occasions, unless your film is a real bomb. I felt I had a lot to be thankful for when we wrapped *Do The Right Thing*. We had a relaxed, practically hassle-free shoot. We had shot an entire film for eight and a half weeks at one location. (What could be easier?) The block residents and the community of Bed-Stuy had given us full cooperation. And the dailies looked good.

A couple of hours before wrap, a bet was waged on the exact time, down to the minute, that we would complete our last shot. One of the drivers won the bet and a pool of forty-five dollars. We broke out the champagne. And after listening to the movie unit cops grumble about permissions, we laid a plaque in front of We Love Radio Station that states that the film was shot on the block. We even put up a street sign renaming Stuyvesant Street "Do The Right Thing Avenue," but the wind blew it down, so it stays in my office now.

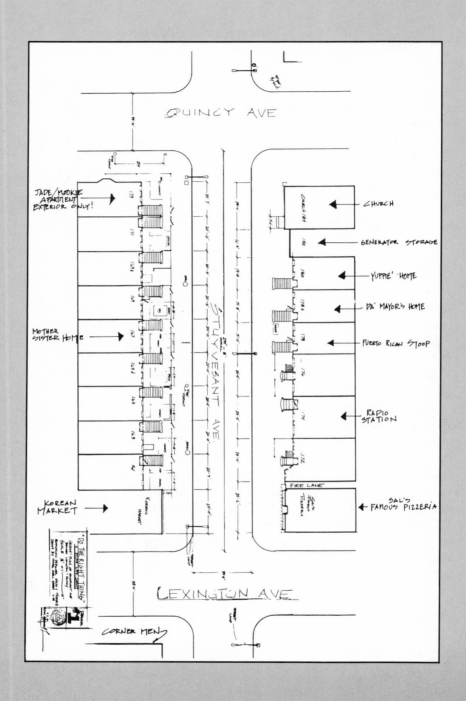

PART III.

THE SCRIPT

It's amazing to me how ideas come. Any time, any place, and whapp! the muse visits. Lightning strikes and it's there. The "it" is that initial kernel that is developed, thought over, and dissected, again and again.

The idea for *Do The Right Thing* arose for me out of the Howard Beach incident. It was 1986, and a Black man was still being hunted down like a dog. Never mind *Mississippi Burning*: Nothing has changed in America, and you don't have to go down south to have a run-in with racist rednecks. They're here in Nueva York.

After Howard Beach, I said to myself, yep, that's it, we're fed up. I think that the only reason a public disturbance didn't jump off was because it was the dead of winter. It was just too damn cold for an uprising. But what if a racial incident like Howard Beach or the Edmund Perry and Eleanor Bumpers murders had happened on the hottest day of the summer?

That "what if" is the basis of *Do The Right Thing*. I decided the entire film had to take place during a twenty-four hour period: a day in the life of one block in the Bedford-Stuyvesant section of Brooklyn, New York.

The first draft was eighty-six pages, lean and mean. Anything that didn't propel the story forward had to go. Initially I wanted a ninety-minute film, but when you start shooting, other things take over. These "other things" account for the now two-hour length of the film. The cliché is true: The movie makes itself, takes on a life of its own, is no longer just words on paper.

While I'm putting the finishing touches on *Do The Right Thing,* I'm thinking about the next Spike Lee joint. Very soon, I'll be getting a visitor. Then wham, presto chango! It's time to start writing again.

DO THE RIGHT THING

by
Spike Lee

Second Draft
March 1, 1988; Brooklyn, N.Y.

Forty Acres and a Mule Filmworks, Inc.
YA-DIG SHO-NUFF
BY ANY MEANS NECESSARY
WGA #45816

"The greatest miracle Christianity has achieved in America is that the black man in white Christian hands has not grown violent. It *is* a miracle that 22 million black people have not *risen up* against their oppressors—in which they would have been justified by all moral criteria, and even by the democratic tradition! It is a miracle that a nation of black people has so fervently continued to believe in a turn-the-other-cheek and heaven-for-you-after-you-die philosophy! It *is a miracle* that the American Black people have remained a peaceful people, while catching all the centuries of hell that they have caught, here in white man's heaven! The *miracle* is that the white man's puppet Negro 'leaders,' his preachers and the educated Negroes laden with degrees, and others who have been allowed to wax fat off their black poor brothers, have been able to hold the black masses quiet until now."

—THE AUTOBIOGRAPHY OF MALCOLM X

TITLES—WHITE ON BLACK

PLACE
Brooklyn, New York

CUT TO:

TIME
Present

CUT TO:

WEATHER
Hot as shit!

CUT TO:

1   **INT:** *WE LOVE RADIO STATION STOREFRONT—DAY*
EXTREME CLOSE UP

WE SEE only big white teeth and very Negroidal *(big)* lips.

MISTER SEÑOR LOVE DADDY

> Waaaake up!
> Wake up! Wake up! Wake up!
> Up ya wake! Up ya wake! Up ya wake!

CAMERA MOVES BACK SLOWLY TO REVEAL MISTER SEÑOR LOVE DADDY, a DJ, a radio personality, behind a microphone.

MISTER SEÑOR LOVE DADDY

> This is Mister Señor Love Daddy.
> Your voice of choice. The world's
> only twelve-hour strongman, here
> on WE LOVE radio, 108 FM. The
> last on your dial, but the first
> in ya hearts, and that's the truth,
> Ruth!

The CAMERA, which is STILL PULLING BACK, shows that Mister Señor Love Daddy is actually sitting in a storefront window. The control booth looks directly out onto the street. This is WE LOVE RADIO, a modest station with a loyal following, right in the heart of the neighborhood. The OPENING SHOT will be a TRICK SHOT —the CAMERA PULLING BACK through the storefront window.

MISTER SEÑOR LOVE DADDY

Here I am. Am I here?
Y'know it. It ya know.
This is Mister Señor Love Daddy,
doing the nasty to ya ears,
ya ears to the nasty.
I'se play only da platters dat matter,
da matters dat platter and
That's the truth, Ruth.

He hits the cart machine and we hear a station jingle.

VO

L-O-V-E RADIO.

MISTER SEÑOR LOVE DADDY

Doing da ying and yang
da flip and flop
da hippy and hoppy
    (he yodels)
Yo da lay he hoo.
I have today's forecast.
(he screams)
HOT!

He laughs like a madman.

2   **INT:** *DA MAYOR'S BEDROOM—DAY*

An old, grizzled man stirs in the bed, his sheets are soaked with sweat. He flings them off his wet body.

DA MAYOR

Damn, it's hot.

3 INT: *JADE'S APARTMENT—DAY*

CAMERA MOVES IN ON a young man sitting at the edge of a sofa bed.

CLOSE UP—HIS SMALL HANDS

WE SEE him counting his money. This isn't any ordinary counting of money, he's straightening out all the corners of the bills, arranging them so the bills—actually the "dead presidents"—are facing the same way. This is MOOKIE. Once he's finished with that task, counting his money, he sneaks into his sister's bedroom.

4 INT: *JADE'S BEDROOM—DAY*

CLOSE UP—JADE

JADE, Mookie's sister, is fast asleep. Mookie's fingers ENTER THE FRAME and start to play with her lips. Jade pushes his hands away. Mookie waits several beats and he continues. Jade wakes up —*mad.*

JADE

Don't you have enough sense not to bother people when they're sleeping?

MOOKIE

Wake up!

JADE

Wake up? Saturday is the lone day I get to sleep late.

MOOKIE

It's gonna be hot today.

JADE

Good! Leave me alone when I'm
sleeping. I'm gonna get a lock
on my door, to keep ya ass outta
here.

MOOKIE

Don't ya love ya brother Mookie
anymore? I loves ya, Jade.

JADE

Do me a favor. Go to work.

MOOKIE

Later. Gotta get paid.

He plants a big fat juicy on his sister's forehead.

5 **EXT:** *SAL'S FAMOUS PIZZERIA—DAY*

A 1975 El Dorado pulls up in front of the neighborhood pizzeria—
Sal's Famous Pizzeria. From out of the car comes the owner, SAL, a
slightly overweight man in his early fifties, and his two sons, PINO,
22, and VITO, 20. It's time for them to go to work at Sal's Famous
Pizzeria in the heart of Black Brooklyn. Sal's sits right on the corner
of The Block. The Block being where this film on the hottest day of
the summer takes place.

Pino kicks a beer can in his path into the gutter.

SAL

Pino, get a broom and sweep
out front.

PINO

Vito, get a broom and sweep
out front.

VITO

See, Pop. That's just what I
was talkin' 'bout. Every single
time you tell Pino to do something,
he gives it to me.

PINO

He's nuts.

SAL

The both of youse, shaddup.

VITO

Tell Pino.

PINO

Get the broom.

VITO

I ain't getting shit.

SAL

Hey! Watch it.

PINO

I didn't want to come to work
anyway. I hate this freakin'
place.

SAL

Can you do better? C'mere.

Pino now is silent. Sal walks over to him.

SAL

Can you do better?
(he pops Pino upside the head)
I didn't think so. This is a
respectable business. Nuthin'
wrong with it. Get dat broom.

PINO

Tell Vito.

VITO

Pop asked you.

SAL

I'm gonna kill somebody today.

6   **EXT:** *MOOKIE'S BROWNSTONE—DAY*

Mookie comes down his stoop and walks to work.

7   **EXT:** *STREET—DAY*

The Block is beginning to come to life. Those unlucky souls who
have to work this Saturday drag themselves to it, and the kids are
out on the street to play in the hot sun all day long.

8   **EXT:** *MOTHER SISTER'S STOOP—DAY*

Mookie stops to say hello to MOTHER SISTER. She leans out her
window on the parlor floor. In the summertime, the only time when
she's not perched in her window is when she's asleep.

MOTHER SISTER

Good morning, Mookie.

MOOKIE

Good morning to you.

MOTHER SISTER

Now, Mookie, don't work too
hard today. The man said it's
gonna be HOT as the devil. I
don't want ya falling out from
the heat. You hear me, son?

MOOKIE

I hear ya, Mother Sister. I
hear you.

MOTHER SISTER

Good. I'll be watching ya, son.
Mother Sister always watches.

9   **INT:** *SAL'S PIZZERIA—DAY*

Mookie enters the pizzeria and Pino is on him before the door closes.

PINO

Mookie, late again. How many
times I gotta tell you?

MOOKIE

Hello, Sal. Hello, Vito.

SAL

How ya doin', Mookie?

VITO

Whaddup?

MOOKIE

Just coolin'.

PINO

You're still late.

SAL

Pino, relax, will ya.

PINO

Here, take the broom. The
front needs sweeping.

MOOKIE

Wait a minute. Wait a minute.
I just got here. You sweep.
I betcha Sal asked you first
anyhow.

VITO

That's right.

PINO

Shaddup, Vito.

MOOKIE

Fuck dat shit. I deliver
pizzas. That's what I get
paid for.

PINO

You get paid to do what we say.

MOOKIE

What *we* say. I didn't hear
Sal say nuthin'.

Pino looks at his father. He wants to be backed up on this; all he
gets is an amused look, and a smirk from Vito.

PINO

Who's working for who?

There's a knock on the door and Da Mayor enters.

SAL

Come on in, Mayor.

DA MAYOR

Good morning, gentlemens. It's
gonna be a scorcher today,
that's for sure. Need any
work done around here?

Sal looks at Pino, who reluctantly gives Da Mayor the broom.

DA MAYOR

It will be the cleanest sidewalk in Brooklyn. Clean as the
Board of Health.

Da Mayor almost runs out of the pizzeria in his hurry; soon as he
finishes he'll be able to get a bottle.

PINO

Pop, I don't believe this shit.
We runnin' welfare or somethin'?
Every day you give dat bum—

MOOKIE

Da Mayor ain't no bum.

PINO

Give dat bum a dollar for
sweeping our sidewalk. What
do we pay Mookie for? He don't
even work. I work harder than
him and I'm your own son.

MOOKIE

Who don't work? Let's see you
carry six large pies up six
flights of stairs. No elevator
either and shit.

SAL

Both of youse—shaddup.
This is a place of business.

VITO

Tell 'em, Pop.

PINO

Me and you are gonna have a
talk.

VITO

Sez who?

PINO

Sez me.

SAL

Hey! What did I say?

MOOKIE

Who doesn't work? Don't start
no shit, won't be no shit.

SAL

Mookie, no cursing in the
store.

MOOKIE

Talk to your son.

10   **EXT:** *SAL'S FAMOUS PIZZERIA—DAY*

Da Mayor sweeps the sidewalk, happy as can be. As soon as he
finishes he can get that money and get that bottle.

11 **EXT:** *STOOP—DAY*

A group of youths sit on a stoop waiting for someone. They are CEE, PUNCHY, and the lone female, ELLA.

ELLA

What's keeping him?

PUNCHY

You call him, then.

Ella stands up and yells.

ELLA

Yo, Ahmad!

PUNCHY

I coulda done dat.

ELLA

Yo, Ahmad!

She looks up into his window, then sits down.

ELLA

Punchy, if ya want to do some
more screaming, be my guest.
I'm *too* through.

The door swings open at the top of the stoop and AHMAD appears.

AHMAD

Who's yelling my name?

Punchy told me to.

AHMAD

Don't listen to him, it will
get ya in trouble.

ELLA

Heard that, Punchy.

Ahmad sits down with them.

AHMAD

Ella, you have a brain,
use it.

In the BG, we hear the dum-dum-dum of a giant box. The sound
gets louder as the box gets closer. The youths look down the block
and see a tall young man coming towards them. He has a very
distinct walk, it's more like a bop. This is RADIO RAHEEM. The
size of his box is tremendous and one has to think, how does he
carry something that big around with him? It must weigh a ton,
and it seems like the sidewalk shakes as the rap music blares out.
The song we hear is the only one Radio Raheem plays.

MEDIUM SHOT—RADIO RAHEEM

Radio Raheem stops in front of the group, looks at them, and turns
down the volume. It's quiet again.

RADIO RAHEEM

Peace, y'all.

ELLA

Peace, Radio Raheem.

133

                              CEE

Peace.

                            PUNCHY

You the man, Radio Raheem.

                            AHMAD

It's your world.

                              CEE

In a big way.

Radio Raheem nods and turns up the volume. Way up.

                            AHMAD

My people. My people.

12   **EXT:** *WE LOVE STOREFRONT—DAY*

Radio Raheem waves to Mister Señor Love Daddy as he walks by.

13   **INT:** *WE LOVE CONTROL BOOTH—DAY*

Mister Señor Love Daddy gives Radio Raheem a clenched-fist salute.

14   **EXT:** *FRUIT-N-VEG DELIGHT—DAY*

Da Mayor walks into a newly opened fruit and vegetable deli stand that is owned by Koreans.

15   **INT:** *FRUIT-N-VEG DELIGHT—DAY*

Da Mayor is looking for his beer in the refrigerated cases, his ice-cold beer.

DA MAYOR

Where's the Bud? Where's the
Bud?

KOREAN CLERK

No mo' Bud. You look what we
have and buy.

DA MAYOR

No more Bud. What kind of joint
is this? How come no mo' Bud?
Doctor, this ain't Korea, China,
or wherever you come from. Get
some Budweiser in this motherfucker.

KOREAN CLERK

You buy 'nother beer.

DA MAYOR

Alright. Alright. Y'know you're
asking a lot to make a man change
his beer, that's asking a lot,
Doctor.

16   **EXT:** *MOTHER SISTER'S STOOP—DAY*

Da Mayor has his can of beer (not Budweiser) and the brown paper
bag is twisted into a knot at the bottom. He stops and takes a long
swig.

MOTHER SISTER

You ole drunk. What did I tell
ya about drinking in front of my
stoop? Move on, you're blocking
my view.

Da Mayor lowers the can from his mouth and looks up at his heck-ler. It's obvious from the look on his face he's heard this before. Da Mayor contorts his face and stares at her.

MOTHER SISTER

You ugly enough. Don't stare
at me.

Da Mayor changes his face into a more grotesque look.

MOTHER SISTER

The evil eye doesn't work on me.

DA MAYOR

Mother Sister, you've been talkin'
'bout me the last eighteen years.
What have I ever done to you?

MOTHER SISTER

You're a drunk fool.

DA MAYOR

Besides that. Da Mayor don't
bother nobody. Nobody don't
bother Da Mayor but you. Da
Mayor just mind his business.
I love everybody. I even love
you.

MOTHER SISTER

Hold your tongue. You don't
have that much love.

DA MAYOR

One day you'll be nice to me.
We might both be dead and buried,
but you'll be nice. At least
civil.

Da Mayor tips his beat-up hat to Mother Sister and takes a final
swig of beer just for her.

16A **INT:** *TINA'S APARTMENT—DAY*

An elderly Puerto Rican woman, CARMEN, is telling off her daughter TINA in Spanish. Tina, having heard enough, closes the door on
her mother's ranting and raving.

ANGLE—*TINA*

Tina bends down and scoops her baby son HECTOR up from the bed
and holds him for dear life to her breasts. She talks to her son while
walking around the room.

TINA

Hector, I shouldn't be telling
you this but you would find
out sooner or later. Ya father
ain't no real father. He's a
bum, a two-bit bum in a hundred-
dollar world. Your father is
to the curb. You're smart.
I see that look on ya face.
You're saying if he's such a
bum why am I with him? Good
question. Like I said
before, you're no dummy.
He talked his way into my
panties, I thought being a
mother would make me happy,
make me whole. He's a mistake,
but you are not.

Tina kisses her son. Tina is seventeen years old, another teenage parent.

17 **EXT:** *STREET CORNER—DAY*

Every day on this corner, summer or winter, spring or fall, a small group of men meet. They have no steady employment, nothing they can speak of; they do, however, have the gift of gab. These men can talk, talk, and mo' talk, and when a bottle is going round and they're feeling "nice," they get philosophical. These men become the great thinkers of the world, with solutions to all its ills; like drugs, the homeless, and AIDS. They're called the Corner Men: SWEET DICK WILLIE, COCONUT SID, and ML. All three are sitting in folding chairs up against a wall in the shade.

> **ML**
>
> The way I see it, if this hot
> weather continues, it will surely
> melt the polar caps and the whole
> wide world—the parts that
> ain't water already—will be
> flooded.

> **COCONUT SID**
>
> You a dumb-ass simple mother-
> fucker. Where did you read
> that?

> **ML**
>
> Don't worry about it. But when
> it happens and I'm in my boat
> and ya black ass is drowning,
> don't ask me to throw you a
> lifesaver either.

SWEET DICK WILLIE

Fool, you're thirty cents away
from a quarter. How you gonna
get a boat?

ML

Don't worry about it.

SWEET DICK WILLIE

You're raggedy as a roach. You
eat the holes out of donuts.

ML

I'll be back on my feet. Soon
enough.

SWEET DICK WILLIE

So when is all this ice suppose
to melt?

18 **INT:** *SAL'S FAMOUS PIZZERIA—DAY*

Customers are in Sal's; it's lunchtime and it's fairly busy. Sal puts
a hot slice down on the counter in front of BUGGIN' OUT, a b-boy.

SAL

You paying now or on layaway?

Buggin' Out looks at the slice.

BUGGIN' OUT

How much?

SAL

You come in here at least three
times a day. You a retard?
A buck fifty.

BUGGIN' OUT

Damn, Sal, put some more cheese
on that motherfucker.

SAL

Extra cheese is two dollars.
Y'know dat.

BUGGIN' OUT

Two dollars! Forget it.

Buggin' Out slams his money down on the counter, takes his slice
and sits down.

ANGLE—*TABLE*

All around Buggin' Out, peering down from the WALL OF FAME,
are signed, framed, eight by ten glossies of famous Italian Ameri-
cans. WE SEE Joe DiMaggio, Rocky Marciano, Perry Como, Frank
Sinatra, Luciano Pavarotti, Liza Minnelli, Governor Mario Cuomo,
Al Pacino and, of course, how can we forget Sylvester Stallone as
Rocky Balboa: THE ITALIAN STALLION, also RAMBO.

CLOSE UP—BUGGIN' OUT

He looks at the pictures hovering above him.

BUGGIN' OUT

Mookie.

CLOSE UP—MOOKIE

MOOKIE

What?

CLOSE UP—BUGGIN' OUT

BUGGIN' OUT

How come you ain't got no
brothers up?

CLOSE UP—MOOKIE

MOOKIE

Ask Sal.

ANGLE—PIZZERIA

BUGGIN' OUT

Sal, how come you ain't got no
brothers up on the wall here?

SAL

You want brothers up on the
Wall of Fame, you open up your
own business, then you can do
what you wanna do. My pizzeria,
Italian Americans up on the wall.

VITO

Take it easy, Pop.

SAL

Don't start on me today.

BUGGIN' OUT

Sal, that might be fine, you
own this, but rarely do I see
any *Italian* Americans eating
in here. All I've ever seen is
Black folks. So since we spend
much money here, we do have some
say.

SAL

You a troublemaker?

Pino walks over to Buggin' Out.

PINO

You making trouble.

BUGGIN' OUT

Put some brothers up on this
Wall of Fame. We want Malcolm X,
Angela Davis, Michael Jordan
tomorrow.

Sal comes from behind the counter with his Louisville Slugger
Mickey Mantle model baseball bat. Vito is by his side, but Mookie
intercepts them, and takes Buggin' Out outside.

SAL

Don't come back, either.

BUGGIN' OUT

Boycott Sal's. Boycott Sal's.

19   **EXT:** *SAL'S PIZZERIA—DAY*

MOOKIE

Buggin' Out, I gotta work here.

BUGGIN' OUT

I'm cool. I'm cool.

MOOKIE

Come back in a week, it will
be squashed.

They give each other five.

20   **INT:** *SAL'S FAMOUS PIZZERIA—DAY*

Mookie enters.

SAL

Mookie, if your friends can't
behave, they're not welcome.

MOOKIE

I got no say over people.

PINO

You talk to 'em.

MOOKIE

People are free to do what
they wanna do.

SAL

I know, this is America, but
I don't want no trouble.

21 **EXT:** *STREET—DAY*

Mookie walks down the block with pizza box in hand when he sees
Da Mayor sitting on his stoop.

DA MAYOR

Mookie.

MOOKIE

Gotta go.

DA MAYOR

C'mere, Doctor.

Mookie turns around and goes back.

DA MAYOR

Doctor, this is Da Mayor
talkin'.

MOOKIE

OK. OK.

DA MAYOR

Doctor, always try to do the
right thing.

MOOKIE

That's it?

DA MAYOR

That's it.

MOOKIE

I got it.

22   **INT:** *TENEMENT BUILDING—DAY*

Mookie is hiking up a flight of stairs.

ANGLE—STAIRCASE

He puts the pizza box down and takes a breather.

CLOSE UP—MOOKIE

Sweat drips off his face.

ANGLE—MOOKIE

He bends down to pick up the pizza box and tackles the last few flights.

CLOSE UP—DOORBELL

Mookie pushes the buzzer.

ANGLE—DOOR

A young Puerto Rican woman opens the door.

NILDA

I hope it's not cold.

Mookie hands her the pizza.

MOOKIE

No, it's not cold. Twelve
dollars for the pie.

Nilda hands him a handful of singles. Mookie looks at the crumpled
mess. Nilda attempts to close the door, but Mookie's foot says, "Hell
no."

MOOKIE

Hold it. Let me count this
first.

First he straightens out the dollars, then counts the bills.

MOOKIE

You're short.

NILDA

I counted the twelve dollars
myself.

MOOKIE

Twelve is right, but no tip.

NILDA

No tip.

MOOKIE

Look, lady. I carried your
pizza up five flights of stairs
and shit. The cheese didn't
slide over to one side like it
sometimes does with delivery

people who don't care. I do
care. May I get paid?

Nilda looks at him and sees right away he's not going anywhere.

NILDA

Wait here.

MOOKIE

I'll wait.

Nilda goes into the apartment and we hear her talking in Spanish
to a male.

ANGLE—MOOKIE

Mookie bends down to tie his sneakers.

ANGLE—DOOR

Nilda reappears and holds out a lonely lone dollar for him. Mookie
has her hold it out for awhile, then he takes it.

MOOKIE

Gracias mucho.

Nilda slams the door.

MOOKIE

A dollar! Cheap bastard!
Your pizza is gonna be fucked
next time.

23   **EXT:** *MOTHER SISTER'S STOOP—DAY*

Jade sits down next to Mother Sister on the stoop.

MOTHER SISTER

Jade, you're late.

JADE

I know, Mother Sister, but I'm
here now. Where's the stuff?

Mother Sister hands her a bag that is at her side.

MOTHER SISTER

Seen your brother, just walked by.

Jade unwraps a head scarf from around Mother Sister's head and a
full head of long black hair falls to her shoulders.

JADE

This might take some time.

MOTHER SISTER

I got nowhere to go. We haven't
had a good sit-down for a long
while.

Jade begins to part, grease, and comb out Mother Sister's hair.

MOTHER SISTER

Tender-headed runs in my family.
You tender-headed?

JADE

Yeah, me too.

MOTHER SISTER

That's why I don't fool with it.
Only let you touch it. . . . Ouch!

JADE

Sorry, comb got caught.

MOTHER SISTER

Be gentle, child. Mother Sister
is an old woman.

JADE

How are you holding up in this
weather?

MOTHER SISTER

I'll do.

JADE

I don't know why you still haven't
bought an air conditioner.

MOTHER SISTER

Don't like 'em. A fan will do.

ANGLE—DA MAYOR

Da Mayor stands in front of the stoop, he's smiling for days.

DA MAYOR

I didn't know you had such
beautiful hair.

ANGLE—STOOP

MOTHER SISTER

Fool, there's a lot in this
world you *don't* know.

CLOSE UP—DA MAYOR

DA MAYOR

I'm not stopping. I'm on my way.

The Mayor tips his hat and heads up the block.

ANGLE—STOOP

JADE

You are too cruel to Da Mayor,
it isn't right.

MOTHER SISTER

I'm not studying no Mayor.
Besides, he reminds me of my
least favorite peoples. My
tenants and my ex-husband—
Goddamn-bless his soul.

They both laugh.

MOTHER SISTER

Number One: I got some jive, late-
rent-paying trifling Negroes in
this house. Every year I keep
threatening to sell it.

JADE

And move to Long Island . . .

MOTHER SISTER

And move to Long Island. Number
two: my ex-husband lost all my
property, all my money in his
scheme to build a Black business
empire. Needless to say what
happened, this house is it, all
I got. I'm too through with yar
people.

CLOSE UP—JADE

JADE

Whew!

She looks up at the white-hot sun.

CLOSE UP—MOTHER SISTER

She does the same.

X CLOSE UP—THE WHITE-HOT SUN

24   HOT, HOTTER AND HOTTEST MONTAGE

Right now, folks, we're gonna suspend the narrative and show how
people are coping with the *oppressive heat.*

People are taking cold showers.

25   Sticking faces in ice-cold, water-filled sinks.

26   Heads stuck in refrigerators.

27 A wife telling her husband, "Hell, no, I'm not cooking. It's too hot. The kitchen is closed."

28 Men downing six-packs of ice-cold brew.

29 Faces stuck directly in front of fans.

29A A young kid cracks an egg on Sal's Cadillac. The moment the egg hits the car hood it starts to cook. The kid looks directly INTO THE CAMERA and smiles, then looks up to see Sal, mad as a mother-fucker, chasing after him.

30 And how can I forget the papers, the newspaper headlines:

> *New York Post:* "A SCORCHER"
> *New York Daily News:* "2 HOT 4 U?'"
> *New York Newsday:* "OH BOY! BAKED APPLE"
> *New York Times:* "RECORD HEATWAVE HITS CITY"

31 **EXT:** *STREET—DAY*

CLOSE UP—JOHNNY PUMP

POW! A powerful gush of water flies out RIGHT AT THE CAMERA.

Ahmad has just turned on the johnny pump and the white stream of water flies across the street.

This attracts all the people of the block. It's a chance to cool off and momentarily beat the *killer heat.*

ANGLE—CEE AND PUNCHY

They both scrape beer cans on the sidewalk.

ANGLE—ELLA

She stands with caution away from the fire hydrant. Ella does not want to get wet.

ANGLE—CEE AND PUNCHY

They're still scraping away.

ANGLE—STREET

Folks, young and old, begin to get in the water and play.

ANGLE—CEE AND PUNCHY

Both now have cans with the ends scraped away, and go to the johnny pump. Punchy bends down behind the hydrant and places the can over the water. The can now directs the water into giant streams.

ANGLE—ELLA

Ahmad sneaks up behind Ella and picks her up. She's kicking and screaming furiously.

ELLA

Ahmad! Put me down! Put me
down! I can't get wet! I'm
not playing!

Ahmad is not having it. He carries a kicking Ella into the middle of the street in direct line of fire.

AHMAD

Yo!

ELLA

No!

They both are hit with a blast of water and are soaked to the bone. Ella starts to punch Ahmad, and chases after him.

ANGLE—STREET

We hear the familiar rap music of Radio Raheem's box.

CLOSE—RADIO RAHEEM

Radio Raheem is too cool. By the way he's dressed, it could be fall, not the *hottest day of the year*. But you could never tell it from him. He's too cool.

CLOSE—RADIO RAHEEM

Raheem looks at Cee, he wants to get by and he doesn't want to get wet either. And if his box gets wet, somebody is gonna die. Cee knows this too.

ANGLE—JOHNNY PUMP

Cee stands in front of the hydrant, blocking the water so Radio Raheem can pass.

ANGLE—RADIO RAHEEM

He slowly bops across the street as all eyes watch. When he's clear, Cee moves and the water gushes out again as folks play.

ANGLE—STREET

We hear a car horn blowing. People move out of the way as the vehicle speeds through the spray.

ANGLE—WHITE CONVERTIBLE

An older man, CHARLIE, stops his white convertible and blows his horn.

CHARLIE
I'm not playing. There's
gonna be trouble if you fuck
around.

CLOSE—CEE AND PUNCHY

PUNCHY
Go 'head. You got it. You
got it.

CLOSE—CHARLIE

CHARLIE

This is an expensive car.

CLOSE—CEE

CEE

You won't get wet.

ANGLE—HYDRANT

Both Punchy and Cee sit in front of the hydrant once again, blocking the water.

ANGLE—WHITE CONVERTIBLE

The car cautiously eases forward. Charlie doesn't trust Cee and Punchy at all.

CLOSE—CHARLIE

CHARLIE

I'm warning you.

CLOSE—CEE AND PUNCHY

PUNCHY

C'mon.

CEE

Hurry up. We ain't got all day.

ANGLE—STREET

The people all move to the car, for they know what is about to happen.

ANGLE—HYDRANT

Cee and Punchy leap off the hydrant, unleashing a jet blast that flies directly into Charlie's car. The whole block is dying.

ANGLE—STREET

Charlie pulls his flooded car over to the curb, jumps out, and runs to get hold of Cee and Punchy. Of course, he's slow, as the kids turn into track stars and make like Carl Lewis.

ANGLE—STREET

Charlie, a wet mess, tries to buy some sympathy from the folks; none is to be bought.

> ### CHARLIE
>
> I'm fucking soaked. If I ever
> catch those fucks they'll be
> sorry. Cocksucking sonabitches!

The ranting continues, and people laugh at him.

> ### CHARLIE
>
> You people make me sick.

A cop car screeches to a halt in front of the man. Two officers, LONG and PONTE, get out.

> ### CHARLIE
>
> Officers, I want an arrest
> made. Now.

> ### OFFICER PONTE
>
> What happened?

CHARLIE

Two Black kids soaked me and
my car. It's fucking ruined.

OFFICER LONG

Where are they?

CHARLIE

Where are they? What kind of
fucking asshole question is
that? They ran the fuck away.

OFFICER PONTE

Do you wish to file a complaint?

CHARLIE

A complaint. I want those fucks
locked *under* the jail.

Officer Long goes into his car and gets a wrench.

ANGLE—JOHNNY PUMP

Officer Long turns off the hydrant, then puts the cap back on.

OFFICER PONTE

This hydrant better not come
back on or there's gonna be
hell to pay.

CHARLIE

What about my car? I want
justice.

Officer Long sides up to Da Mayor who's been looking on.

OFFICER LONG

You know anything about this?

Da Mayor is quiet.

CHARLIE

He knows. He's a witness.
They all know. He saw the whole thing.

Officer Ponte goes to Da Mayor's other side.

OFFICER LONG

Who were the punks?

DA MAYOR

Those who'll tell don't know.
Those who know won't tell.

OFFICER PONTE

A wise guy.

Mookie emerges from the crowd and leads Da Mayor away from the interrogation.

MOOKIE

Let's go, Mayor.

OFFICER LONG

Keep this hydrant off. You
want to swim, go to Coney
Island.

CHARLIE

He's leaving? What about me?

OFFICER PONTE

I suggest you get in your car
quick, before *these people*
start to strip it clean.

The man looks at the crowd of Blacks and Puerto Ricans around
him and he considers what he just heard.

OFFICER LONG

Let's go, break it up. Go back
to your jobs.

OFFICER PONTE

What jobs?

Both cops laugh.

ANGLE—STREET

Charlie drives away, fuming.

33 INT: *ROOFTOP—DAY*

Cee and Punchy look down from a roof on all the havoc and confusion they've started. Both laugh.

33 **INT:** *SAL'S FAMOUS PIZZERIA—DAY*

Mookie enters.

> ### SAL
>
> Mookie, what took you so long?
> I got a business to run.

> ### MOOKIE
>
> Run it then.

> ### SAL
>
> Here, this goes to the radio
> station.

He gives Mookie a bag full of food.

> ### VITO
>
> Pop, I'm gonna go with Mookie.

> ### SAL
>
> Good, make sure he don't jerk
> around.

> ### PINO
>
> Yeah, hurry back, it's getting
> crowded.

34 **EXT:** *STREET—DAY*

Vito and Mookie walk down the block.

VITO

Mister Señor Love Daddy is
cool.

MOOKIE

Ya like him, huh?

VITO

Yeah.

MOOKIE

Y'know, Vito, I know Pino is
ya brother and shit, but the
next time he hits ya, the next
time he touches ya, you should
"house him." Kick his ass.

VITO

I don't know.

MOOKIE

If you don't make a stand, he's
gonna be beating ya like a egg
for the rest of your life.

VITO

That's what you think?

MOOKIE

That's what I think.

VITO

I don't like to fight.

MOOKIE

Do it this one time and he'll
never touch you again.

35   **EXT:** *WE LOVE RADIO—DAY*

Mookie and Vito wave at Mister Señor Love Daddy through the
storefront window and he buzzes them in.

36   OMIT

37   **INT:** *CONTROL BOOTH—DAY*

Mookie and Vito very quietly walk in; the man is on the air.

MISTER SEÑOR LOVE DADDY

Peoples, my stomach's been
grumbling but help has arrived.
My main man Mookie has saved
the day, straight from Sal's
Famous Pizzeria, down the
block. Come up to the mike, Mookie.

Mookie goes to the mike.

MISTER SEÑOR LOVE DADDY

C'mon, don't be shy. Mmm,
smells good. This is ya Love
Daddy talkin' to ya, starvin'
like Marvin. Say something,
Mookie.

MOOKIE

Mister Señor Love Daddy, I'd
like to dedicate the next record
to my heart, Tina.

MISTER SEÑOR LOVE DADDY

Alright. Let me play this record
while I go to work on my chicken
Parmigiana hero with extra cheese
and extra sauce.

He hits the cart machine . . .

VO

I just looove you so much
Mister Señor Love Daddy.
WE LOVE RADIO, 108 FM.

. . . then cues up the record.

MISTER SEÑOR LOVE DADDY

Here ya are.
(he hands Mookie a twenty-dollar bill)
Keep the change.

MOOKIE

That's right on time. This is
my friend, Vito. His pops is
Sal.

MISTER SEÑOR LOVE DADDY

Tell ya father he makes the
best heros in Brooklyn.

VITO

I'll do that.

MOOKIE

We're outta here.

MISTER SEÑOR LOVE DADDY

Thanks for stopping by.
WE LOVE Radio, 108 FM.

38 **EXT:** *STREET—DAY*

On a stoop, a group of Puerto Ricans sits talking, drinking *cerveza frío,* and playing dominoes. One of their cars is parked near the stoop, and blasts salsa music.

ANGLE—RADIO RAHEEM

As usual we hear the rap music of Radio Raheem, but underneath the salsa music. Radio Raheem does not like to be bested; the salsa music from the parked car is giving him competition, this is no good. Radio Raheem stands in front of the stoop and raises his decibel level.

ANGLE—STOOP

The Puerto Rican men look at him, then begin to yell at him in Spanish. There is a standoff, the rap and salsa clashing in a deafening roar. One of the men, STEVIE, gets off the stoop and goes to the car.

ANGLE—CAR

Stevie turns the car radio off.

CLOSE—RADIO RAHEEM

Radio Raheem smiles, nods, turns his box to a reasonable listening level, and bops down the block. Radio Raheem still the loudest. Radio Raheem still the king.

STEVIE

You got it, bro.

ANGLE—STOOP

The men curse in Spanish and shake their heads in bewilderment
and Stevie turns the salsa back on.

39   **EXT:** *STREET—DAY*

Vito and Mookie see Buggin' Out on their way back to Sal's.

MOOKIE

You the man.

BUGGIN' OUT

You the man.

MOOKIE

No, you the man.

BUGGIN' OUT

No. I'm just a struggling Black
man trying to keep my dick hard
in a cruel and harsh world.

Buggin' Out gives Mookie five and a menacing look at Vito.

MOOKIE

Vito is down.

40   **EXT:** *STREET—DAY*

Buggin' Out is walking down the block when CLIFTON, a yuppie,
accidentally bumps into him, stepping on his new sneakers.

CLOSE—BUGGIN' OUT

He looks at his sneakers.

CLOSE—SNEAKERS

There is a big black smudge on his new white unlaced Air Jordans.

ANGLE—BUGGIN' OUT

He runs down the block after Clifton.

> **BUGGIN' OUT**
> Yo!

Clifton turns around.

> **BUGGIN' OUT**
> Yo!

> **CLIFTON**
> Yes?

> **BUGGIN' OUT**
> You almost knocked me down.
> The word is "excuse me."

> **CLIFTON**
> Excuse me. I'm very sorry.

> **BUGGIN' OUT**
> Not only did you knock me down,
> you stepped on my new white

Air Jordans that I just bought
and that's all you can say,
"Excuse me"?

This commotion has attracted a crowd, including Ahmad, Cee, Punchy, and Ella.

BUGGIN' OUT

I'll fuck you up quick two times.

HERE WE GO!

BUGGIN' OUT

Who told you to step on my
sneakers? Who told you to walk
on my side of the block? Who
told you to be in my neighborhood?

CLIFTON

I own a brownstone on this block.

BUGGIN' OUT

Who told you to buy a brownstone on my block, in my
neighborhood on my side of the
street?

The crowd likes that one and they laugh and egg him on.

BUGGIN' OUT

What do you want to live in a
Black neighborhood for? Motherfuck
gentrification.

CLIFTON

I'm under the assumption that
this is a free country and one
can live where he pleases.

BUGGIN' OUT

A free country?

AWWW SHIT! Why did he get Buggin' started?

BUGGIN' OUT

I should fuck you up just for
that stupid shit alone.

Buggin' Out looks down at his marred Air Jordans. The crowd,
smelling blood, wants to see some.

AHMAD

Your Jordans are dogged.

CEE

You might as well throw 'em
out.

PUNCHY

They looked good before he
messed them up.

ELLA

You used to be so fine.

AHMAD

How much did you pay for them?

CEE

A hundred bucks.

AHMAD

A hundred bucks!

BUGGIN' OUT

You're lucky the Black man has
a loving heart. Next time you
see me coming, cross the
street quick.

AHMAD

He's dissing you.

BUGGIN' OUT

Damn, my brand-new Jordans.
You should buy me another pair.

CLIFTON

I'm gonna leave now.

BUGGIN' OUT

If I wasn't a righteous Black
man you'd be in serious trouble.
SERIOUS.

The crowd gives their approval.

BUGGIN' OUT

Move back to Connecticut.

41 INT: *SAL'S FAMOUS PIZZERIA—DAY*

Mookie and Vito enter the shop.

SAL

I should have Vito go with you
all the time.

PINO

Yeah, no more ninety-minute
deliveries around the corner.

MOOKIE

Pino, I work hard like everybody
in here.

VITO

He's right.

PINO

C'mere.
         (Pino smacks his brother)
Don't get too friendly with
da Mook.

SAL

That's gonna be the last time
you hit Vito.

MOOKIE

Smack him back.

PINO

What?

MOOKIE

Remember what I said.

Vito stands frozen in front of his brother.

PINO

Are you gonna listen to this
Mook? Listen to him tell you
to smack me? Your only
brother?

Vito walks away and Mookie is disgusted.

PINO

I didn't think so.

42   **EXT:** *STREET—DAY*

Officers Ponte and Long drive down the block and at the corner they
stop, glare at the Corner Men.

CLOSE—OFFICER PONTE

CLOSE—SWEET DICK WILLIE

CLOSE—OFFICER LONG

CLOSE—COCONUT SID

ANGLE—POLICE CAR

OFFICER PONTE

What a waste.

ANGLE—CORNER

Sweet Dick, ML, and Coconut Sid stare right back at the cops.

ANGLE—POLICE CAR

It drives off.

ANGLE—CORNER

COCONUT SID

As I was saying before we were
so rudely interrupted by the
finest.

ML

What was you saying?

Coconut Sid blanks.

SWEET DICK WILLIE

Motherfucker wasn't saying shit.

ML

Look at that.

COCONUT SID

Look at what?

ML points across the street to the Korean fruit and vegetable stand.

ML

It's a fucking shame.

SWEET DICK WILLIE

What is?

ML

Sweet Dick Willie.

SWEET DICK WILLIE

That's my name.

ML

Do I have to spell it out?

COCONUT SID

Make it plain.

ML

OK, but listen up. I'm gonna
break it down.

SWEET DICK WILLIE

Let it be broke.

ML

Can ya dig it?

SWEET DICK WILLIE

It's dug.

CLOSE—ML

ML

Look at those Korean motherfuckers across the street. I
betcha they haven't been a year
off da motherfucking boat before
they opened up their own place.

CLOSE—COCONUT SID

COCONUT SID

It's been about a year.

CLOSE—ML

ML

A motherfucking year off the
motherfucking boat and got a
good business in our neighborhood
occupying a building that
had been boarded up for longer
than I care to remember and
I've been here a long time.

CLOSE—SWEET DICK WILLIE

SWEET DICK WILLIE

It has been a long time.

CLOSE—COCONUT SID

COCONUT SID

How long?

CLOSE—ML

ML

Too long! Too long. Now for
the life of me, I haven't been
able to figger this out. Either
dem Koreans are geniuses or
we Blacks are dumb.

This is truly a stupefying question and all three are silent. What is the answer?

COCONUT SID

It's gotta be cuz we're Black.
No other explanation, nobody
don't want the Black man to
be about shit.

SWEET DICK WILLIE

Old excuse.

ML

I'll be one happy fool to see
us have our own business right
here. Yes, sir. I'd be the
first in line to spend the
little money I got.

Sweet Dick Willie gets up from his folding chair.

SWEET DICK WILLIE

It's Miller time. Let me go
give these Koreans s'more
business.

ML

It's a motherfucking shame.

COCONUT SID

Ain't that a bitch.

43 **EXT:** *STOOP—DAY*

Da Mayor sits on his stoop and a kid, EDDIE, runs by.

DA MAYOR

Sonny! Sonny!

Eddie stops.

DA MAYOR

Doctor, what's your name?

EDDIE

Eddie Lovell.

DA MAYOR

How old are you?

EDDIE

Ten.

DA MAYOR

What makes Sammy run?

EDDIE

My name is Eddie.

DA MAYOR

What makes Sammy run?

EDDIE

I said my name is Eddie Lovell.

DA MAYOR

Relax, Eddie, I want you to go
to the corner store. How
much will it cost me?

EDDIE

How would I know how much it's
gonna cost if I don't know
what I'm buying?

DA MAYOR

Eddie, you're too smart for
your own britches. Listen
to me. How much do you want
to run to the store for Da
Mayor?

EDDIE

Fifty cents.

DA MAYOR

You got a deal.

He gives Eddie some money.

DA MAYOR

Git me a quart of beer, Budweiser,
say it's for your father, if
they bother you.

Eddie runs down the block just as Ahmad, Cee, Punchy, and Ella pass him.

AHMAD

Who told him he was Da Mayor
of this block?

CEE

He's self-appointed.

ELLA

Leave him alone.

PUNCHY

Shut up.

DA MAYOR

Go on now. Leave me be.

AHMAD

You walk up and down this block
like you own it.

CEE

Da Mayor.

PUNCHY

You're old.

AHMAD

A old drunk bum.

Da Mayor stands up from his seat cushion on the stoop.

AHMAD

What do you have to say?

DA MAYOR

What do you know 'bout me?
Y'all can't even pee straight.
What do you know? Until you
have stood in the doorway and
heard the hunger of your five
children, unable to do a damn
thing about it, you don't
know shit. You don't know
my pain, you don't know me.
Don't call me a bum, don't
call me a drunk, you don't
know me, and it's disrespectful.
I know your parents raised you
better.

The teenagers look at Da Mayor.

ELLA

He told you off.

Da Mayor sits back down on his seat cushion on his stoop.

44 INT: *SAL'S FAMOUS PIZZERIA—DAY*

ANGLE—PAY PHONE ON WALL

Mookie is on the phone.

MOOKIE

I know I haven't seen you in
four days. I'm a working man.

TINA (VO)

I work too, but I still make time.

MOOKIE

Tina, what do you want me to
do?

TINA (VO)

I want you to spend some time
with me. I want you to try and
make this relationship work.
If not, I'd rather not be
bothered.

MOOKIE

Alright. Alright. I'll be
over there sometime today.

TINA (VO)

When?

MOOKIE

Before I get off work.

TINA (VO)

Bring some ice cream, I'm
burning up. Do you love me?

MOOKIE

Do I love you?

CLOSE—SAL

SAL

Mookie, get offa da phone.

CLOSE—MOOKIE

MOOKIE

Be off in a second. Tina, I
dedicated a record on Mister
Señor Love Daddy's show to you.

TINA (VO)

Big deal.

CLOSE—SAL

SAL

Mookie! How is anybody gonna
call in?

CLOSE—MOOKIE

MOOKIE

Big deal? If that's not LOVE,
I don't know what is.

CLOSE—PINO

PINO

You deaf or what?

CLOSE—MOOKIE

MOOKIE

Gotta go. See ya soon.
(he hangs up)
Everybody happy now?

The phone rings right away and Pino picks it up.

ANGLE—PINO

PINO

Sal's Famous Pizzeria, yeah,
two large pizzas, pepperoni and
anchovies, hold on. . . . See,
Pop, Mookie fucking talking on
the phone and people are trying
to call in orders. He's making
us lose business.

CLOSE—SAL

SAL

Mookie, you're fucking up.

PINO

Twenty minutes.
(he hangs up the phone)
How come you niggers are so
stupid?

CLOSE—MOOKIE

                              MOOKIE
    If ya see a nigger here, kick
    his ass.

CLOSE—PINO

                              PINO
    Fuck you and stay off the phone.

CLOSE—VITO

                              VITO
    Forget it, Mookie.

ANGLE—PIZZERIA

                              MOOKIE
    Who's your favorite basketball
    player?

                              PINO
    Magic Johnson.

                              MOOKIE
    And not Larry Bird? Who's your
    favorite movie star?

                              PINO
    Eddie Murphy.

Mookie is smiling now.

MOOKIE

Last question: Who's your
favorite rock star?

Pino doesn't answer, because he sees the trap he's already fallen
into.

MOOKIE

Barry Manilow?

Mookie and Vito laugh.

MOOKIE

Pino, no joke. C'mon, answer.

VITO

It's Prince. He's a Prince
freak.

PINO

Shut up. The Boss! Bruuucce!!!!

MOOKIE

Sounds funny to me. As much as
you say nigger this and nigger
that, all your favorite people
are "niggers."

PINO

It's different. Magic, Eddie,
Prince are not niggers, I mean,
are not Black. I mean, they're

Black but not really Black.
They're more than Black. It's
different.

With each word Pino is hanging himself even further.

MOOKIE

Pino, I think secretly that
you wish you were Black. That's
what I think. Vito, what do
you say?

PINO

Y'know, I've been listening and
reading 'bout Farrakhan, ya didn't
know that, did you?

MOOKIE

I didn't know you could read.

PINO

Fuck you. Anyway, Minister
Farrakhan always talks about
the so-called "day" when the
Black man will rise. "We will
one day rule the earth as we
did in our glorious past."
You really believe that shit?

MOOKIE

It's e-vit-able.

PINO

Keep dreaming.

MOOKIE

Fuck you, fuck pizza, and fuck
Frank Sinatra, too.

PINO

Well, fuck you, too, and fuck
Michael Jackson.

CUT TO:

RACIAL SLUR MONTAGE
The following will be a QUICK-CUTTING MONTAGE of racial
slurs, with different ethnic groups pointing the finger at one another. Each person looks directly INTO THE CAMERA.

45 CLOSE—MOOKIE

MOOKIE

Dago, wop, garlic-breath, guinea,
pizza-slinging, spaghetti-
bending, Vic Damone, Perry
Como, Luciano Pavarotti, Sole
Mio, nonsinging motherfucker.

CUT TO:

46 CLOSE—PINO

PINO

You gold-teeth, gold-chain-
wearing, fried-chicken-and-
biscuit-eatin', monkey, ape,
baboon, big thigh, fast-running,
three-hundred-sixty-degree-
basketball-dunking spade
Moulan Yan.

~

CUT TO:

47 CLOSE—STEVIE

STEVIE

You slant-eyed, me-no-speak-
American, own every fruit and
vegetable stand in New York,
Reverend Moon, Summer
Olympics '88, Korean kick-
boxing bastard.

CUT TO:

48 CLOSE—OFFICER LONG

OFFICER LONG

Goya bean–eating, fifteen in a
car, thirty in an apartment,
pointed shoes, red-wearing,
Menudo, meda-meda Puerto Rican
cocksucker.

CUT TO:

49 CLOSE—KOREAN CLERK

KOREAN CLERK

It's cheap, I got a good price
for you, Mayor Koch, "How I'm
doing," chocolate-egg-cream-
drinking, bagel and lox, B'nai
B'rith asshole.

CUT TO:

50 **INT:** *WE LOVE RADIO STATION CONTROL ROOM—DAY*

CLOSE—MISTER SEÑOR LOVE DADDY

MISTER SEÑOR LOVE DADDY

Yo! Hold up! Time out! Time
out! Y'all take a chill. Ya
need to cool that shit out . . .
and that's the truth, Ruth.

CUT TO:

X CLOSE—WHITE-HOT SUN

51 **INT:** *SAL'S FAMOUS PIZZERIA—DAY*

Mookie picks up his two pizza pies for delivery.

MOOKIE

Sal, can you do me a favor?

SAL

Depends.

MOOKIE

Can you pay me now?

SAL

Can't do.

MOOKIE

Sal, just this once, do me
that solid.

SAL

You know you don't get paid
till we close tonight. We're
still open.

MOOKIE

I would like to get paid now.

SAL

Tonight, when we close.

Mookie leaves.

52   **EXT:** *STREET—DAY*

Mookie walks down the block. The streets are filled with kids playing. WE SEE stoop ball, double dutch, hand games, bike-riding,
skateboarding, etc.

ANGLE—MOOKIE

Radio Raheem approaches Mookie.

MOOKIE

Whaddup. Money?

RADIO RAHEEM

I was going to buy a slice.

MOOKIE

I'll be back after I make this
delivery.

RADIO RAHEEM

On the rebound.

Mookie stares at the gold "brass knuckles" rings Radio Raheem wears on each hand. Spelled out across the rings are the words "LOVE" on the right hand and "HATE" on the left hand.

MOOKIE

That's the dope.

RADIO RAHEEM

I just copped them. Let me
tell you the story of Right-Hand—
Left-Hand—the tale of Good
and Evil.

MOOKIE

I'm listening.

RADIO RAHEEM

HATE!

He thrusts up his left hand.

RADIO RAHEEM

It was with this hand that Brother
Cain iced his brother. LOVE!

He thrusts up his right hand.

RADIO RAHEEM

See these fingers, they lead straight
to the soul of man. The right hand.
The hand of LOVE!

Mookie is buggin'.

RADIO RAHEEM

The story of Life is this . . .

He locks his fingers and writhes, cracking the joints.

RADIO RAHEEM

STATIC! One hand is always
fighting the other. Left Hand Hate
is kicking much ass and it looks
like Right Hand Love is finished.
Hold up. Stop the presses! Love
is coming back, yes, it's Love.
Love has won. Left Hand Hate
KO'ed by Love.

Mookie doesn't know what to say, so he doesn't say anything.

RADIO RAHEEM

Brother Mookie, if I love you I
love you, but if I hate you . . .

MOOKIE

I understand.

RADIO RAHEEM

I love you, my brother.

MOOKIE

I love you, Black.

53 **INT:** *SAL'S PIZZERIA—DAY*

Radio Raheem enters Sal's with music blaring.

RADIO RAHEEM

Two slices.

SAL

No service till you turn dat
shit off.

RADIO RAHEEM

Two slices.

PINO

Turn it off.

SAL

Mister Radio Raheem, I can't
even hear myself think. You
are disturbing me and you are
disturbing my customers.

Sal grabs his Mickey Mantle bat from underneath the counter.
Everyone, Sal, Vito, Pino, Radio Raheem, and the customers are
poised for something to jump off, STATIC.

CLOSE—RADIO RAHEEM

He smiles and turns off the beat.

RADIO RAHEEM

Two slices, extra cheese.

CLOSE—SAL

Sal puts Mickey Mantle back into its place.

When you come in Sal's Famous
Pizzeria, no music. No rap,
no music. Capisce? Understand?
. . . This is a place of business.
Extra cheese is two dollars.

54   INT: *TENEMENT HALLWAY—DAY*

Mookie hands the pizzas over and takes the money and counts it.

MOOKIE

Thanks.

55   EXT: *STREET—DAY*

Mookie walks, says hello to the people he knows.

56   EXT: *STOOP—DAY*

Mookie runs up stoop.

57   INT: *MOOKIE'S APARTMENT—DAY*

We hear a key in the door, the lock turns and Mookie enters.

MOOKIE

Jade.

JADE (OS)

I'm in here.

58   INT: *JADE'S BEDROOM—DAY*

Jade sits in a chair directly in front of an air conditioner going full blast.

JADE

How come you're not at Sal's?

MOOKIE

I'm working.

JADE

Is this another one of your patented two-hour lunches?

MOOKIE

I just come home to take a quick shower.

JADE

Sal's gonna be mad.

MOOKIE

Later for Sal. Y'know, sometimes I think you're more concerned with him than me.

JADE

I think no such a thing. Sal pays you, you should work.

MOOKIE

Slavery days are over. My name ain't Kunta Kinte. Sis,

I don't want to argue, stop
pressing me.

JADE

I just don't want you to lose
the one job you've been able to
keep, that's all. I'm carrying
you as it is.

MOOKIE

Don't worry 'bout me. I always
get paid.

JADE

Yeah, then ya should take better
care of *your* responsibilites.

MOOKIE

What responsibilities?

JADE

I didn't stutter. Take care of
your responsibilities. Y'know
exactly what I'm talking about.

59   **INT:** *BATHROOM—DAY*

Mookie turns on the shower and screams; the water is ice cold.

60   **EXT:** *MOTHER SISTER'S STOOP—DAY*

Mother Sister sits in her window looking out at the block.

61   **EXT:** *DA MAYOR'S STOOP—DAY*

Da Mayor has fallen asleep sitting on his stoop. His hands loosely hold a brown paper bag that is tightly twisted around a beer can.

62 **EXT:** *CORNER—DAY*

Sweet Dick, ML, and Coconut Sid each hold an umbrella for protection from the hot and harsh rays.

63 **EXT:** *FIRE ESCAPE—DAY*

Ahmad, Punchy, Cee, and Ella sit on a fire escape, trying to keep still, trying to find a cool spot in the shade. No one says a word.

64 **INT:** *SAL'S FAMOUS PIZZERIA—DAY*

Sal takes a seat at one of the tables.

> **SAL**
>
> I'm beat.

Pino sits down next to his father.

> **PINO**
>
> Pop, I think we should sell
> this place, get outta here
> while we're still ahead . . .
> and alive.

> **SAL**
>
> Since when do you know what's
> best for us?

> **PINO**
>
> Couldn't we sell this and open
> up a new one in our own neigh-
> borhood?

SAL

Too many pizzerias already
there.

PINO

Then we could try something
else.

SAL

We don't know nuthin' else.

PINO

I'm sick of niggers, it's a
bad neighborhood. I don't
like being around them, they're
animals.

VITO

Some are OK.

PINO

My friends laugh at me all
the time, laugh right in my
face, tell me go feed the
Moulies.

SAL

Do your friends put money in
your pocket? Pay your rent?
Food on ya plate?

Pino is quiet.

                              SAL

I didn't think so.

                             PINO

Pop, what else can I say? I
don't wanna be here, they don't
want us here. We should stay
in our own neighborhood, stay
in Bensonhurst.

                              SAL

So what if this is a Black
neighborhood, so what if we're
a minority. I've never had no
trouble with dese people, don't
want none either, so don't
start none. This is America.
Sal's Famous Pizzeria is here
for good. You think you know
it all? Well, you don't. I'm
your father, you better remember
that.

65   **INT:** *BATHROOM—DAY*

Mookie pulls the shower curtain back and steps out.

66   **INT:** *MOOKIE'S ROOM—DAY*

Mookie sits on his bed, still wet.

ANGLE—JADE

                             JADE

Hurry up and get dressed.

MOOKIE

I'm coming.

JADE

I'm going with you.

66A BUGGIN' OUT BOYCOTT MONTAGE

EXT: *STREET—DAY*

BUGGIN' OUT

Da Mayor, we need your
leadership.

DA MAYOR

Doctor, what are you
talkin' bout?

BUGGIN' OUT

I'm organizing a boycott
of Sal's Famous Pizzeria.

DA MAYOR

Keep walkin', Doctor. I don't
want to hear none of your
foolishness.

CUT TO:

CLOSE—CORNER MEN

ML

No!

COCONUT SID

No!

SWEET DICK WILLIE

Hell no! Goddamnit. Sal
ain't never done me no
harm. You either.

CUT TO:

CLOSE—BUGGIN' OUT

BUGGIN' OUT

Would you like to sign a
petition to boycott Sal's
Famous Pizzeria?

CUT TO:

CLOSE—AHMAD, CEE, PUNCHY, and ELLA

They DOG him out (ADLIB)

CUT TO:

CLOSE—BUGGIN' OUT

BUGGIN' OUT

I'll do it without your
help.

67 **EXT:** *WE LOVE RADIO—DAY*

Buggin' Out waves at Mister Señor Love Daddy as he walks by the
storefront.

68 **INT:** *SAL'S FAMOUS PIZZERIA—DAY*

Buggin' Out sticks his head in and yells:

> #### BUGGIN' OUT
>
> Sal, we're gonna boycott ya
> fat ass.

Before Sal and his two sons can answer, Buggin' Out is gone.

69 **EXT:** *STREET—DAY*

Buggin' Out has one foot up on a fire hydrant and tries to clean his
soiled Air Jordan.

ANGLE—JADE AND MOOKIE

Jade and Mookie walk up to Buggin' Out.

> #### BUGGIN' OUT
>
> It's so nice to see a family
> hanging out together.

> #### MOOKIE
>
> We're not hanging out. I'm
> being escorted back to work.

> #### JADE
>
> That's not even true. I just
> want a slice.

> #### BUGGIN' OUT
>
> Jade, you don't know this, but
> I'm organizing a boycott of
> Sal's Famous Pizzeria.

JADE

What did he do this time?

BUGGIN' OUT

Y'know all those pictures he
has hanging on the Wall of
Fame?

JADE

So?

BUGGIN' OUT

Have you noticed something
about them?

JADE

No.

MOOKIE
(interjects)

Yo, I'm gone.

JADE

I'll see ya there.

BUGGIN' OUT

Peace.

Mookie leaves.

BUGGIN' OUT

Every single one of those
pictures is somebody Italian.

JADE

And?

BUGGIN' OUT

And I—we—want some Black people
up.

JADE

Did you ask Sal?

BUGGIN' OUT

Yeah, I asked him. I don't want
nobody in there, nobody spending
good money in Sal's. He should
get no mo' money from the
community till he puts some
Black faces up on that motherfucking wall.

Jade looks at Buggin' Out like "Are you serious?"

JADE

Buggin' Out, I don't mean to be
disrespectful, but you can
really direct your energies in
a more useful way.

BUGGIN' OUT

So, in other words, you are not
down.

JADE

I'm down, but for a worthwhile
cause.

BUGGIN' OUT

Jade, I still love you.

JADE

I still love you too.

INT: *SAL'S FAMOUS PIZZERIA—DAY*

SAL

Mookie, you are pushing it.
You're really pushing it. I'm
not paying you good money to
fucking jerk me around.

Mookie has nothing to say.

SAL

You're gonna be in the street
with the rest of your homeboys.

PINO

'Bout time, Pop.

ANGLE—DOOR

Jade enters, and Sal looks up. He stops blasting Mookie and a very
noticeable change comes over him.

SAL

Jade, we've been wondering when
ya would pay us a visit.

JADE

Hi, Sal, Pino, Vito.

VITO

What's happening, Jade?

JADE

Nuthin' really. How are you
treating my brother?

SAL

The Mook? Great. Mookie's a
good kid.

PINO

Pop, stop lying.

SAL

Shaddup! Jade, what can I
fix you?

JADE

What's good?

SAL

Everything, but for you I'm
gonna make up something special.
Take a seat. There, that's a
clean table.

Sal moves behind the counter and goes to work. Pino and Mookie
look at each other in agreement, neither likes what he has seen.
This happens to Sal every time Jade is in Sal's Famous Pizzeria.

ANGLE—TABLE

Vito sits down with Jade.

JADE

You still letting Pino push
you around?

VITO

Who told you that? He doesn't
push me, who told you, Mookie tell
you that? I hold my own.

JADE

Forget about it, Vito. Forget
I *even* brought it up.

VITO

Pino picks on me, but I don't
let him push me around. Mookie
tell you that?

JADE

Alright already.

71 **EXT:** *ROOFTOP—DUSK*

The once white-hot sun is now turning into a golden orange glaze as it begins to set. Ahmad, Cee, Punchy, and Ella dance on the roof around a box that is turned into WE LOVE. Each one is trying to come up with some new moves, a new dance, and a name for it.

72 **EXT:** *STREET—DUSK*

Radio Raheem is walking down the block and there is something wrong, something is not quite right. AHA! His music is not loud; the rap song begins to drag and finally stops altogether.

CLOSE—RADIO RAHEEM

He looks at his box and presses the battery level indicator.

CLOSE—BATTERY LEVEL INDICATOR

The needle doesn't move. His batteries have had it.

73 **INT:** *FRUIT-N-VEG DELIGHT—DUSK*

CLOSE—RADIO RAHEEM

RADIO RAHEEM
Twenty "D" Duracells.

CLOSE—KOREAN CLERK

KOREAN CLERK
Twenty "C" Duracells.

CLOSE—RADIO RAHEEM

RADIO RAHEEM
D, not C.

CLOSE—KOREAN CLERK

KOREAN CLERK

C Duracell.

CLOSE—RADIO RAHEEM

RADIO RAHEEM

D! D! D! You dumb motherfucker.
Learn how to speak English first.
D.

Radio Raheem points to the D batteries behind the counter.

CLOSE—KOREAN CLERK

KOREAN CLERK

How many you say?

CLOSE—RADIO RAHEEM

RADIO RAHEEM

Twenty! Motherfucker! Twenty!

CLOSE—KOREAN CLERK

KOREAN CLERK

Motherfucker you.

Radio Raheem has to laugh at that one.

RADIO RAHEEM

Motherfucker you. You're
alright. You're alright. Just
gimme my twenty Duracells, please.

74 **EXT:** *FRUIT-N-VEG DELIGHT—DUSK*

Da Mayor is looking at a bunch of cut flowers when Radio Raheem comes out with batteries in hand—finally.

75 **EXT:** *MOTHER SISTER'S STOOP—DUSK*

ANGLE—WINDOW

Mother Sister is sitting in her window as usual.

ANGLE—STOOP

Da Mayor walks up the stoop with a bunch of fresh-cut flowers in a discarded wine bottle for a vase.

ANGLE—DA MAYOR

Da Mayor holds them out for Mother Sister, who does not acknowledge him at all.

> **DA MAYOR**
>
> I'd thought you might like
> these. . . . I guess not.

Da Mayor takes a seat on the stoop and puts the flowers to his face.

> **DA MAYOR**
>
> Ain't nuthin' like the smell
> of fresh flowers. Don't you
> agree, Miss Mother Sister?

Mother Sister does not answer. He puts the flowers down.

> **DA MAYOR**
>
> Summertime, all ya can smell
> is the garbage. Stink overpowers
> everything, especially soft sweet
> smells like flowers.

He looks up at Mother Sister who immediately turns away.

DA MAYOR

If you don't mind, I'm gonna
set right here, catch a breeze
or two, then be on my way.

Da Mayor looks up at the setting sun.

DA MAYOR

Thank the Lord, the sun is
going down, it's hot as blazes.
Yes Jesus.

CLOSE—SUN

The sun is an orange and purple glaze.

76   **EXT:** *STREET—DUSK*

Radio Raheem is back in action. He's alive, he's bad and he got his
twenty "D" Duracell batteries, his box is kicking.

ANGLE—CORNER

Radio Raheem bops by Coconut Sid, ML, and Sweet Dick Willie.

CLOSE—COCONUT SID, ML, and SWEET DICK WILLIE

All three shake their heads in bewilderment as Radio Raheem goes
by.

ML

What can you say?

COCONUT SID

I don't know how he does it.

Sweet Dick Willie gets up from his chair and goes to the corner, zips down his pants, and urinates.

SWEET DICK WILLIE

ML?

ML

What?

SWEET DICK WILLIE

ML, hold this for me.

Sweet Dick Willie and Coconut Sid laugh.

ML

That's OK. At least my moms
didn't name me Sweet Dick Willie.

Sweet Dick Willie zips up his pants and returns to his seat.

SWEET DICK WILLIE

Why you gotta talk 'bout my
moms?

ML

Nobody talkin' 'bout ya moms.

SWEET DICK WILLIE

I didn't say *nobody,* I said *you.*

ML

Sweet Dick, I didn't mean it like
that.

SWEET DICK WILLIE

Yes you did.

COCONUT SID

Squash it.

ML

I just wanted to know who named
ya Sweet Dick Willie?

SWEET DICK WILLIE

It's just a name.

COCONUT SID

And what does ML stand for?

ML

ML stands for ML. That's it.

SWEET DICK WILLIE

Naw, that's some stupid shit.
Now you know how I got that name.

ML

Negroes kill me, always holdin'
onto, talkin' 'bout their dicks.

COCONUT SID

I don't know 'bout you, but it's
too hot to fuck.

SWEET DICK WILLIE

Never too hot, never too cold
for fucking.

77 **EXT:** *STREET—DUSK*

An old Puerto Rican man rings a bell as he pushes a cart on wheels.
On the side of the cart is hand-lettered HELADO DE COCO, and a
big block of ice rests on top surrounded by different colored bottles
of flavors.

ANGLE—CART

A group of kids eagerly waits for the ices. The man scrapes the
block of ice, puts the shavings in a paper cup, and drowns it with
syrup.

ANGLE—DA MAYOR

Da Mayor is walking down the street.

ANGLE—MISTER SOFTEE TRUCK

We hear the familiar tune from the Mister Softee truck as it comes
down the street.

ANGLE—EDDIE LOVELL

Eddie, the young kid who earlier ran an errand for Da Mayor, looks
up from the sidewalk where he's playing and runs out into the street
in pursuit of Mister Softee.

EDDIE

Ice cream. Ice cream.

Eddie is running in pursuit of the truck, unaware of the oncoming speeding car.

ANGLE—DA MAYOR

Da Mayor sees speeding car bearing down on Eddie.

ANGLE—STREET

Da Mayor runs across the street and knocks Eddie down, out of the way of the car. Both are thrown as they are hit by the reckless driver.

CLOSE—EDDIE AND DA MAYOR

Eddie is crying as Da Mayor picks him up.

DA MAYOR

> Doctor, you know better to run
> out in the street. . . . Stop
> crying, son.

ANGLE—STREET

A crowd gathers.

DA MAYOR

> Doctor, there's nothing to cry
> about. You're OK.

A woman in her twenties, LOUISE, Eddie's mother, breaks through the crowd and hugs her baby.

LOUISE

> What's wrong?

EDDIE

> Mayor knocked me down.

LOUISE

You should be ashamed of yourself.

DA MAYOR

Ma'am, the boy is just scared
to death. What actually
happened is that I was minding
my business when I saw your son
about to be run over. I ran
into the street to save him
and I had to knock him down to
keep the both of us from getting
hit.

The crowd agrees "That's the way it happened," and Louise stands
up.

LOUISE

Eddie, is that the truth?

Eddie is quiet.

LOUISE

Eddie, you hear me talkin' to
you?

Eddie is still mum.

LOUISE

I'm talkin' to you, boy.

DA MAYOR

Miss, the boy is fine.

WHAP! Louise hits Eddie on da butt. Eddie starts to dance, as his mother hits hard; she's heavy-handed.

LOUISE

What I tell you 'bout
lying?

WHOP!

LOUISE

What did I tell you 'bout
playing in the street?

WHAP!

EDDIE

Mommy! Mommy! I'm sorry.
I'm sorry.

WHOP!

LOUISE

Get upstairs now.

Eddie runs away.

LOUISE

And when your father comes home,
he's gonna wear ya little narrow
behind out too.

DA MAYOR

You didn't have to hit your son;
he's scared to death as it was.

LOUISE

I appreciate ya helping my Eddie.
I truly do, but I'll have nobody
question how I raise him, not
even his Daddy.

DA MAYOR

You're right.

Louise goes away, probably to give her son another "whooping." Da
Mayor tips his hat to her.

78 **INT:** *SAL's FAMOUS PIZZERIA—DUSK*

Sal sits at a table talking to Jade as she finishes her "special" slice.

JADE

Sal, that was delicious.

SAL

Anytime.

Vito, Pino, and Mookie look on, watching Sal have the time of his
life.

JADE

Thanks.

Jade gets up and Mookie helps her.

MOOKIE

I'll see you out.

JADE

See ya around.

SAL

Don't wait too long to come
back.

79   **EXT:** *SAL'S FAMOUS PIZZERIA—DUSK*

Mookie takes Jade by the hand and pulls her out of view from Sal.

ANGLE—MOOKIE AND JADE

MOOKIE

Jade, I don't want you coming
in here no mo'.

JADE

Stop tripping.

MOOKIE

No, you're tripping. Don't
come in Sal's. Alright, read
my lips.

JADE

What are you so worked up about?

MOOKIE

Over Sal, the way he talks and
the way he looks at you.

JADE

He's just being nice.

MOOKIE

Nice!

JADE

He's completely innocent.

MOOKIE

Innocent!

JADE

I didn't stutter. You heard me.

MOOKIE

You should see the way he
looks at you. All Sal wants
to do is hide the salami.

JADE

You are too crude.

MOOKIE

I might be, but you're not
welcome here.

JADE

Stop trying to play big brother.
I'm a grown woman. You gotta

lotta nerve. Mookie, you can hardly pay your rent and you're gonna tell me what to do. Come off it.

MOOKIE

One has nuthin' to do with the other.

JADE

Oh, it doesn't, huh! You got your little 250 dollars a week plus tips . . .

MOOKIE

I'm getting paid . . .

JADE

. . . peanuts.

MOOKIE

Pretty soon I'll be making a move.

JADE

I truly hope so. I'm tired of supporting a grown man.

80 **INT:** *CONTROL BOOTH—DUSK*

CLOSE—MISTER SEÑOR LOVE DADDY

MISTER SEÑOR LOVE DADDY

As the evening slowly falls
upon us living here in Brooklyn,
New York, this is ya Love Daddy
rappin' to you. Right now we're
gonna open up the Love Lines.
Hello, you're on Love Daddy's
Love Line. No names, please.
Let's keep it anonymous.

FEMALE VOICE #1 (VO)

Hi, Mister Señor Love Daddy.
I'd kiss your feet every morning,
that's how much I love you.

MISTER SEÑOR LOVE DADDY

How nice of you.

FEMALE VOICE #2 (VO)

I think you have the sexiest
voice in the world. All you
have to do is talk.

MISTER SEÑOR LOVE DADDY

Love Line, you're on.

FEMALE VOICE #3 (VO)

You give me fever.
                    (she moans)

MISTER SEÑOR LOVE DADDY

She's feeling it.

FEMALE VOICE #4 (VO)

Love Daddy, I'd work in Mickey
D's 24, 7, and 365 just to call
you my own. Give you all my
money, honey.

MISTER SEÑOR LOVE DADDY

That was the last call for
tonight on Mister Señor Love
Daddy's Love Line. I love you.
You I love.

81   **EXT:** *MOTHER SISTER'S STOOP—NIGHT*

Da Mayor is walking by Mother Sister in her window when she
calls him.

CLOSE—MOTHER SISTER

MOTHER SISTER

Mister Mayor, I saw what you
did.

ANGLE—DA MAYOR

Da Mayor stops and looks at her. A smile comes to his face; after
eighteen years has he finally broken down her defenses?

CLOSE—MOTHER SISTER

MOTHER SISTER

That was a foolish act, but
it was brave. That chile owes
you his life.

CLOSE—DA MAYOR

DA MAYOR

I wasn't trying to be a hero.
I saw what was about to happen
and I reacted, didn't even
think. If I did, I might not
have done it in second thought.
Da Mayor is an old man, haven't
run that fast in years. I
went from first to home on a
bunt single, scored the winning
run, the bottom of the ninth,
two out, August 1, 1939, Snow
Hill, Alabama.
                    (he is warming up now)
Maybe I should be heroic more
often.

CLOSE—MOTHER SISTER

MOTHER SISTER

Maybe you shouldn't. Don't
get happy. This changes nothing
between you and me. You did a
good thing and Mother Sister
wanted to thank you for it.

ANGLE—STOOP

DA MAYOR

I thank you.

MOTHER SISTER

You're welcome.

Da Mayor tips his hat.

82 **INT:** *SAL'S FAMOUS PIZZERIA—NIGHT*

Mookie enters.

MOOKIE

Sal, I don't care if you fire
me this exact minute, leave
my sister alone.

SAL

Mookie, I don't know what
you're talking about, plus I
don't want to hear it.

MOOKIE

Sal, just do me a favor, leave
Jade alone.

SAL

Here, you gotta delivery.

Mookie takes the pie and looks at the address.

MOOKIE

Is this the right name and
address?

SAL

Yeah, do you know 'em?

MOOKIE

No, just checking.

83 **INT:** *HALLWAY—NIGHT*

Mookie rings the bell and a fine Puerto Rican sister answers the door.

MOOKIE

Delivery from Sal's Famous
Pizzeria.

TINA

What took you so long? Is it hot?

MOOKIE

Hot. Hot.

TINA

Come in then.

84 **INT:** *TINA'S APARTMENT—NIGHT*

Tina watches Mookie watch her. When she's through watching, she takes the pizza from his hands and puts it on the floor. Mookie grabs her and starts to kiss. Tina is Mookie's woman, the one he's been on the phone with earlier. We've heard the voice and now SEE the person.

MOOKIE

Tina, you are *too* slick.

TINA

How else was I going to get
you here? I haven't seen you
in a week.

MOOKIE

I've been working hard, getting
paid.

TINA

Where's the ice cream? The
Häagen-Dazs butter pecan?

MOOKIE

Shit! I forgot.

TINA

Your memory is really getting
bad.

MOOKIE

I just forgot.

TINA

And I really wanted some ice
cream too.

MOOKIE

I can run out and get it.

TINA

No! No! You won't come back
either.

MOOKIE

I can't be staying long anyway.

TINA

How long then?

MOOKIE

Long enough for us to do the
nasty.

TINA

That's out. No! It's too hot!
You think I'm gonna let you get
some, put on your clothes, then
run outta here and never see you
again in who knows when?

MOOKIE

A quickie is good every once in
a blue moon.

TINA

You a blue-moon fool.

MOOKIE

Then we'll do something else.

TINA

What else?

MOOKIE

Trust me.

TINA

Trust you? Because of trusting
you we have a son. Remember your
son?

MOOKIE

Trust me.

Mookie pushes Tina back into her bedroom.

85 **INT:** *TINA'S BEDROOM—NIGHT*

Mookie sits Tina down on her futon bed, turns off the lights, and
turns on WE LOVE RADIO as Mister Señor Love Daddy serenades
them with slow jams.

MOOKIE

I'm gonna take off ya clothes.

TINA

Mookie, I told you already it's
too fucking hot to make love.

MOOKIE

Why you gotta curse?

TINA

I'm sorry, but no rawness is
jumping off tonight.

MOOKIE

No rawness.

He laughs his sinister laugh.

ANGLE—MOOKIE AND TINA

Mookie unsnaps her bra, then pulls her panties off. Tina is naked as a jaybird.

> **MOOKIE**
>
> Tina, you're sweating.

> **TINA**
>
> Of course I'm sweating. I'm
> burning up. It's hot, moron,
> only a hundred degrees in here.

> **MOOKIE**
>
> Lie down, please.

He gets up.

86 **INT:** *TINA'S KITCHEN*

Mookie walks into the kitchen and sees CARMEN, Tina's mother, fixing some food on the stove.

> **MOOKIE**
>
> Hello, Mrs. Rampolla.

Carmen stares at him, it's a look that would definitely stop traffic, she mutters some Spanish and goes into her bedroom, slamming the door behind her.

ANGLE—MOOKIE

He opens the refrigerator and takes out all the trays of ice.

87   **INT:** *TINA'S BEDROOM—NIGHT*

Mookie sits down on the bed with a bowl filled with ice cubes.

CLOSE—TINA'S FOREHEAD

Mookie rubs an ice cube on her forehead.

> **TINA**
>
> It's cold.

> **MOOKIE**
>
> It's 'pose to be cold.

> **TINA**
>
> Later for you.

> **MOOKIE**
>
> Meda. Meda.

> **TINA**
>
> What?

> **MOOKIE**
>
> Tina, you don't have a forehead,
> you got a eight-head.

CLOSE—TINA'S NECK

Mookie rubs an ice cube on her neck.

CLOSE—TINA'S LIPS

Mookie rubs an ice cube on her full moist lips, then puts it in her mouth.

MISTER SEÑOR LOVE DADDY (VO)

Yes, children, this is the
Cool Out Corner. We're slowing
it down for all the lovers in
the house. I'll be giving you
all the help you need, musically,
that is.

CLOSE—TINA'S THIGHS

He rubs an ice cube up and down her thighs.

MOOKIE (VO)

Thank God for thighs.

CLOSE—TINA'S BUTTOCKS

He rubs an ice cube on her round, firm buttocks.

MOOKIE (VO)

Thank God for buttocks.

CLOSE—TINA'S BREAST

He rubs an ice cube on her breast.

MOOKIE (VO)

Thank God for the right nipple . . .
Thank God for the left nipple . . .

Both Tina and Mookie are dying. Mookie now has an ice cube on
the left and right nipples and WE SEE before our very own eyes
both get swollen, red, and erect.

TINA (VO)

Feels good.

MOOKIE (VO)

Yes, yes, Lord. Isn't this
better than Haagen-Dazs butter
pecan ice cream?

CLOSE—TINA'S MOUTH

Mookie kisses her.

MOOKIE

I'll be back tonight.

88   INT: *SAL'S FAMOUS PIZZERIA—NIGHT*

Officers Ponte and Long are awaiting their orders.

SAL

It's almost ready.

OFFICER LONG

What time you closing tonight?

SAL

Ten.

Sal goes over to the oven, takes out their food and wraps it up.

SAL

Here you go.

OFFICER PONTE

What do we owe you?

SAL

Nine-fifty.

OFFICER PONTE

Here.

SAL

Thanks. Enjoy.

OFFICER LONG

Vito, Pino, see ya later.

The officers leave just as Mookie enters.

MOOKIE

Sal, if you want me to deliver
any faster, get me a jet
rocket or something, cuz I
can't run with pizzas, all the
cheese ends up on one side and
shit.

SAL

I didn't say nuthin'. You
must have a guilty conscience.
What are you guilty of?

MOOKIE

I'm not guilty of nuthin'.

SAL

You must be guilty of something
or you would have never come
in saying the things you said.

MOOKIE

C'mon, Sal.

SAL

Where we goin'?

While Sal laughs at his corny joke, Pino pulls Vito into the back.

89   **INT:** *STOREROOM—NIGHT*

PINO

Vito, I want you to listen
to me. I'm your brother. I
may smack you around once in
awhile, boss you around, but
I'm still your brother.

VITO

I know this.

PINO

I love you.

VITO

I'm listening.

PINO

Good. I want you to listen.

VITO

Jesus Christ on the cross, I
said I'm listening.

PINO

Good. Vito, you trust that
Mook too much. So does Pop.

VITO

Mookie's OK.

PINO

You listening to me?

VITO

Stop busting my balls. I said
I'm listening ten fucking times
already.

PINO

Mookie is not to be trusted.
No Moulan Yan can be trusted.
The first time you turn your
back, boom, a knife right
here.
      (Pino gestures)
In the back.

VITO

How do you know this?

PINO

I know.

VITO

You really think so?

PINO

I know so. He, them, they're
not to be trusted.

VITO

So what do you want me to do?

PINO

Be on guard. Mookie has Pop
conned already, so *we* have to
look out for him.

VITO

I like Mookie a lot.

PINO

And that's exactly what I'm
talkin' 'bout.

SAL (OS)

Vito! Pino! Let's go.

PINO

Be right there, Pop. Listen
to what I said.

VITO

You don't listen to me, never
have. Just run your big fucking
mouth always playing big brother.
You don't listen, but Mookie does.

90   HOT CITY NIGHT MONTAGE

THE BLOCK. WE'VE SEEN it at daytime, but now WE SEE it at
night. Even though the white-hot sun is gone, nonetheless the heat
is still stifling. And in a peculiar, funny sort of way, it's worse. You
expect it to be hot during the light of day when the sun is beating
down on the cement and tar, but at night it should be considerably
cooler; well, not tonight, *it's hot*. All the residents of The Block: the
Corner Men, Mother Sister, Da Mayor, Jade, etc., all the people
WE'VE SEEN throughout the day are now coping with the nighttime heat, plus it's *humid as shit*. Everyone is outside, sitting on
stoops, on cars and you know the kids are playing, running up and
down the block. Now it's *the hottest night of the year*.

91   EXT: *STREET—NIGHT*

Buggin' Out sits down on a car next to Radio Raheem; as usual, his
box is blasting.

BUGGIN' OUT

How you be?

RADIO RAHEEM

I be. I'm living large.

BUGGIN' OUT

Is that the only tape you got?

RADIO RAHEEM

You don't like Public Enemy?
It's the dope shit.

BUGGIN' OUT

I like 'em, but you don't play
anything else.

RADIO RAHEEM

I don't like anything else.

BUGGIN' OUT

Check this out. Y'know Sal's.

RADIO RAHEEM

Yeah, I know dat motherfucker.

BUGGIN' OUT

I'm trying to organize a
boycott of Sal's pizza joint.
Ya see what I'm saying?

RADIO RAHEEM

I almost had to yoke him this
afternoon. Tell me, tell me,
Radio Raheem, to turn my music
down. Didn't even say please.
Who the fuck he think he is?
Don Corleone and shit.

BUGGIN' OUT

He makes all his money off us
Black people and I don't see

nuthin' but Italians all up
in there, Sylvester Stallone
and motherfuckers. Ya see what
I'm saying, homeboy?

RADIO RAHEEM

Talk to me.

BUGGIN' OUT

We shouldn't buy a single slice,
spend a single penny in that
motherfucker till some people
of color are put up in there.

RADIO RAHEEM

That's what I'm talkin' 'bout.
That's what I'm talkin' 'bout.

BUGGIN' OUT

You got my back.

RADIO RAHEEM

Ya back is got.

BUGGIN' OUT

My brother.

RADIO RAHEEM

My brother.

92 INT: *SAL'S PIZZERIA—NIGHT*

Vito, Pino and Mookie are cleaning up.

MOOKIE

Sal, it's almost quitting time
so please start counting my
pay. I gotta get paid.

Sal is looking into the cash register.

SAL

We did good business today.
We got a good thing going.
Nothing like a family in
business working together.
One day the both of you will
take over . . . and Mookie, there
will always be a place for you
at Sal's Famous Pizzeria.
Y'know, it should be Sal's and
Sons Famous Pizzeria.

ANGLE—VITO, PINO, AND MOOKIE

All three look at each other. The horror is on their faces, with the
prospect of working, slaving in Sal's and Sons Famous Pizzeria,
trapped for the rest of their lives. Is this their future? It's a frightening thought.

ANGLE—DOOR

Ahmad, Cee, Punchy, and Ella enter.

SAL

We're about to close.

AHMAD

Just four slices, regular
slices. Please. To go!

SAL

OK, but that's it. It's been
a long day.

Mookie goes over to the table where Ahmad, Cee, Punchy, and Ella
sit.

MOOKIE

Look, I want you to get your
slices, then outta here. No
playing around.

AHMAD

You got it.

MOOKIE

Good. No joke. We all wanna
go home.

OH NO! We hear the dum-dum-dum of Radio Raheem's box. As
everyone turns their heads to the door, Buggin' Out and Radio
Raheem are inside already. We have never heard the rap music as
loud as it is now. You have to scream to be heard and that's what
they do.

SAL

What did I tell ya 'bout dat noise?

BUGGIN' OUT

What did I tell ya 'bout dem
pictures?

SAL

What da fuck! Are you deaf?

BUGGIN' OUT

No, are you? We want some
Black people up on the Wall
of Fame.

SAL

Turn that JUNGLE MUSIC off.
We ain't in Africa.

Ahmad, Cee, Punchy, and Ella start to dance while Mookie takes a
seat, the impartial observer that he is.

BUGGIN' OUT

Why it gotta be about jungle
music and Africa?

SAL

It's about turning that shit
off and getting the fuck outta
my pizzeria.

PINO

Radio Raheem.

RADIO RAHEEM

Fuck you.

SAL

What ever happened to nice
music with words you can
understand?

RADIO RAHEEM

This is music. My music.

VITO

We're closed.

BUGGIN' OUT

    You're closed alright, till
    you get some Black people up
    on that wall.

Sal grabs his Mickey Mantle bat from underneath the counter and brings it down on Radio Raheem's box, again and again and again. The music stops.

CLOSE—RADIO RAHEEM'S BOX.

Radio Raheem's pride and joy is smashed to smithereens. It's going to the junkyard quick.

ANGLE—PIZZERIA

There is an eerie quiet as everyone is frozen, surprised by the suddenness of Sal's action, the swings of his Mickey Mantle bat. All look at Radio Raheem and realize what is about to happen.

ANGLE—RADIO RAHEEM

Radio Raheem screams, he goes crazy.

RADIO RAHEEM

    My music!

Radio Raheem picks Sal up from behind the counter and starts to choke his ass. Radio Raheem's prized possession—his box, the only thing he owned of value—his box, the one thing that gave him any sense of worth—has been smashed to bits. (Radio Raheem, like many Black youth, is the victim of materialism and a misplaced sense of values.) Now he doesn't give a fuck anymore. He's gonna make Sal pay with his life.

Vito and Pino jump on Radio Raheem, who only tightens his grip around Sal's neck. Buggin' Out tries to help his friend. Mookie just stands and watches as Ahmad, Cee, Punchy, and Ella cheerlead.

93   **EXT:** *SAL'S FAMOUS PIZZERIA—NIGHT*

The tangled mass of choking, biting, kicking, screaming confusion flies through the door of Sal's out onto the sidewalk.

CLOSE—EDDIE

The kid yells:

                         EDDIE
            Fight! Fight!

                                              CUT TO:

CLOSE—DA MAYOR

He looks up.

                                              CUT TO:

CLOSE—MOTHER SISTER

She looks up.

                                              CUT TO:

CLOSE—SWEET DICK WILLIE

He also looks up.

ANGLE—STREET

The people on The Block run to Sal's Famous Pizzeria to see the STATIC.

ANGLE—SAL'S FAMOUS PIZZERIA

Radio Raheem, Buggin' Out, Sal, Vito, and Pino are still entangled, rolling around on the sidewalk, but now before an entertained crowd of onlookers:

ANGLE—DA MAYOR

DA MAYOR

Break it up. This is crazy.

The fight continues. Da Mayor is smart enough not to get in the middle of this war. We hear sirens, somebody has called DA COPS.

ANGLE—STREET

The cop cars come right through the crowd, almost running over some people. The cops get out with nightsticks and guns drawn. WE RECOGNIZE two of the faces, Officers Long and Ponte. Any time there is a skirmish between a Black man and a white man, you can bet the house on who the cops are gonna go for. You know the deal! Buggin' Out is pulled off first, then Vito and Pino, but Radio Raheem is a crazed man. It takes all six cops to pull him off Sal, who is red as a beet from being choked.

ANGLE—COPS

Handcuffs are put on Buggin' Out as he watches the other cops put a choke hold on Radio Raheem to restrain him.

ANGLE—RADIO RAHEEM

Radio Raheem is still struggling, then he just stops, his body goes limp and he falls to the sidewalk like a fifty-pound bag of Idaho potatoes.

ANGLE—STREET

Officers Long and Ponte kick him.

OFFICER LONG

Get up! Get up!

Radio Raheem just lies there like a bump on a log.

ANGLE—CROWD

The crowd stares at Radio Raheem's still body. He's unconscious or dead.

CLOSE—OFFICER LONG

OFFICER LONG

Quit faking.

ANGLE—STREET

The officers all look at each other. They know, they know exactly what they've done. *The infamous Michael Stewart choke hold.*

OFFICER PONTE

Let's get him outta here.

The officers pick up Radio Raheem's limp body and throw him into the back seat. Buggin' Out is pushed into another car. The cop cars speed off; in their haste to beat it, they have left the crowd. It's at this point the crowd becomes an angry *mob*.

ANGLE—MOB

The mob looks at . . .

ANGLE—MOB POV

Sal still on the sidewalk, being helped to his feet by Vito and Pino, who are in bad shape themselves.

ANGLE—MOB

The mood/tone of the mob is getting ugly. Once again they have seen one of their own killed before their eyes at the hands of the cops. We hear the murmurs of the folks go through the crowd.

VOICES OF MOB

THEY KILLED HIM
THEY KILLED RADIO RAHEEM
IT'S MURDER
DID IT AGAIN
JUST LIKE THEY DID MICHAEL STEWART
MURDER
ELEANOR BUMPERS
MURDER
IT'S NOT SAFE
NOT EVEN IN OUR OWN NEIGHBORHOOD
IT'S NOT SAFE
NEVER WAS
NEVER WILL BE

The cops, in their haste to get Radio Raheem out of there, have left an angry mob of Black folks with a defenseless Sal, Vito, and Pino.

The mob looks at them.

VOICES OF MOB

WON'T STAND FOR IT
THE LAST TIME
FUCKIN' COPS
THE LAST TIME
IT'S PLAIN AS DAY
DIDN'T HAVE TO KILL THE BOY

HIGH ANGLE

Mookie looks at the crowd and notices he's on the wrong side. He leaves Sal and his two sons.

ANGLE—STREET

Da Mayor walks in front of the crowd.

DA MAYOR

Good people, let's all go home.
Somebody's gonna get hurt.

CROWD (OS)

Yeah, you!

DA MAYOR

If we don't stop this now, we'll
all regret it. Sal and his two
boys had nothing to do with what
the police did.

CROWD (OS)

Get out of the way, old man.
You a Tom anyway.

DA MAYOR

Let 'em be.

ANGLE—STREET

Mookie picks up a garbage can and dumps it out into the street. He
walks through the crowd, up to Da Mayor, Sal, Vito, and Pino.

CLOSE—MOOKIE

He screams.

MOOKIE

HATE!!!!

SLOW MOTION

Mookie hurls the garbage can through the plate glass window of
Sal's Famous Pizzeria. *That's it. All hell breaks loose.* The dam has

been unplugged, broke. The rage of a people has been unleashed, a fury. A lone garbage can thrown through the air has released a tidal wave of frustration.

ANGLE—STREET

Da Mayor pushes Sal, Vito, and Pino out of the way as the mob storms into Sal's Famous Pizzeria.

94   **INT:** *SAL'S FAMOUS PIZZERIA—NIGHT*

The people rush into Sal's Famous Pizzeria, tearing it up.

CLOSE—CASH REGISTER

The cash register is opened. WE SEE only coins, Sal has the paper.

95   **EXT:** *DA MAYOR'S STOOP—NIGHT*

Da Mayor leads Sal, Vito, and Pino back to his stoop where they watch in horror.

SAL

There it goes. Why?

DA MAYOR

You was there. First white
folks they saw. You was there.

PINO

Fuckin' niggers.

96   **INT:** *SAL'S FAMOUS PIZZERIA—NIGHT*

Someone lights a match. WHOOOSH!

97   **EXT:** *SAL'S FAMOUS PIZZERIA—NIGHT*

Sal's Famous Pizzeria is going up in flames 'and now it's a carnival.

MOTHER SISTER

Burn it down. Burn it down.

One might have thought that the elders—who through the years have been broken down, whipped, their spirits crushed, beaten into submission—would be docile, strictly onlookers. That's not true except for Da Mayor. The rest of the elders are right up in it with the young people.

98 **INT:** *SAL'S FAMOUS PIZZERIA—NIGHT*

CLOSE—PHOTOS ON WALL OF FAME

The photos of famous Italian-Americans are burning.

99 **EXT:** *FRUIT-N-VEG DELIGHT—NIGHT*

The mob now moves across the street in front of the Korean fruit and vegetable stand. Sweet Dick Willie, Coconut Sid, and ML stand at the head of the mob.

ML

It's your turn.

CLOSE—KOREAN CLERK

He's scared to death, as the mob is poised to tear his place up too. The clerk wildly swings a broom to hold them off.

KOREAN CLERK

Me no white. Me no white.
Me Black. Me Black. Me Black.

CLOSE—ML

ML

Me Black. Me Black.

The mob starts to laugh; they feel for him.

ANGLE—MOB

SWEET DICK WILLIE

Korea man is OK. Let's leave
him alone.

ML

Him no white. Him no white.

COCONUT SID

Him Black. Him Black.

100   **EXT:** *DA MAYOR'S STOOP—NIGHT*

Sal, Vito, and Pino look on as Sal's Famous Pizzeria goes up in
smoke.

                                        DISSOLVE TO:

CLOSE—VITO

                                        DISSOLVE TO:

CLOSE—PINO

                                        DISSOLVE TO:

CLOSE—SAL

101   **EXT:** *STREET—NIGHT*

ANGLE—STREET

Jade is running through the mob, looking for her brother.

JADE

Mookie! Mookie!

ANGLE—MOOKIE

Mookie is running around with the rest of the mob.

ANGLE—STREET

The wail of fire trucks and police sirens is now added to the night.

102   **EXT:** *SAL'S FAMOUS PIZZERIA—NIGHT*

The mob moves back to in front of Sal's as the fire trucks and police, in full riot gear, pull up in the street behind them.

POLICE LOUDSPEAKER (VO)

Good people. Please disperse.
Please disperse.

The firemen rush to hook up their hoses, the police force themselves between the crowd and the burning Sal's Famous Pizzeria.

POLICE LOUDSPEAKER (VO)

Please disperse! Please
disperse!

The mob doesn't listen, they will not be moved. The mob will not be moved until they see Sal's Famous Pizzeria burn to the ground.

ANGLE—SAL'S FAMOUS PIZZERIA

The firemen douse the pizzeria, trying desperately to stop the fire from spreading into the adjoining buildings.

POLICE LOUDSPEAKER (VO)

Good people, we're giving you one
more warning. Please go back
home.

CLOSE—MOOKIE

MOOKIE

This is our home.

CLOSE—MOTHER SISTER

MOTHER SISTER

This is our neighborhood.

ANGLE—MOB

It will take force to move this mass of people.

POLICE LOUDSPEAKER (VO)

You've had your warning!

POW!

The hoses are turned on the mob.

WE SEE Mookie, Mother Sister, Sweet Dick Willie, ML, Coconut
Sid, Jade, Ahmad, Cee, Punchy, and Ella, etc., go down before the
powerful blast of the firehoses.

*Now we've come full circle. We're back to Montgomery or Birming-
ham, Alabama. The only thing missing is Sheriff Bull Connor and
the German shepherds.*

It would take force to move them and that's exactly what the mob
got. People are trying to hold on to each other, cars, railings, anything to keep from being swept away.

103   **EXT:** *DA MAYOR'S STOOP—NIGHT*

Da Mayor, Sal, Vito, and Pino watch in disbelief. It's unbelievable what is happening before their eyes.

CUT TO:

104   THE STREET—NIGHT
THEIR POV

People are screaming, kids and women are not being spared from the brute force of the firehoses either.

105   **EXT:** *WE LOVE STOREFRONT—NIGHT*

WE SEE the reflection of the fire in the storefront window as Mister Señor Love Daddy looks on.

106   **EXT:** *STREET—NIGHT*

ANGLE—JADE AND MOTHER SISTER

Jade and Mother Sister try to hold on to a streetlamp as a gush of water hits them; their grip loosens, the water is too powerful, and they slide away down the block and Da Mayor runs after them.

107   **INT:** *SAL'S FAMOUS PIZZERIA—NIGHT*

CLOSE—PHOTOS

Some burnt photos on the floor.

CLOSE—MICKEY MANTLE BAT

The Mickey Mantle bat burns.

CLOSE—RADIO RAHEEM'S BOX

Radio Raheem's box has melted into a black mass of goo.

CLOSER—RADIO RAHEEM'S BOX

As WE MOVE IN TIGHTER ON the melted box, we begin to hear the rap song that we've heard throughout. All other sound drops as the rap song gets louder and louder until it's deafening.

107A   ANGLE—SMILEY

Smiley sits up from where he hid during the burning and looting of Sal's Famous Pizzeria. Smiley looks around and goes directly to the smoldering Wall of Fame. He stands there. Smiley pins one of his Malcolm X/Martin Luther King, Jr., cards to the Wall of Fame.

CLOSE—PHOTO

CLOSE—SMILEY

We're on Smiley's face and a smile slowly travels across. It's the first time Smiley has smiled in years and nobody is there to see this event.

FADE TO BLACK

THE MORNING AFTER

FADE IN:

108   **EXT:** *THE STREET—TO INT: RADIO STATION STORE-FRONT—DAY*

The CAMERA, FROM HIGH ABOVE, CRANES DOWN ON The Block. The sidewalk is deserted, broken glass is everywhere, and it looks exactly as how one expects it to look, the morning after an uprising.

The CAMERA NOW MOVES IN ON the WE LOVE storefront where Mister Señor Love Daddy is in his familiar place behind the mike.

MISTER SEÑOR LOVE DADDY

My people. My people.
What can I say?
Say what I can.
I saw it but I didn't believe it.
I didn't believe it what I saw.
Are we gonna live together?
Together are we gonna live?
This is ya Mister Señor Love Daddy
here on WE LOVE RADIO, 108 FM
on your dial, and that's the truth,
Ruth.

CLOSE—MISTER SEÑOR LOVE DADDY

MISTER SEÑOR LOVE DADDY

Today's weather.
(he yells)
HOT!

CLOSER—MISTER SEÑOR LOVE DADDY

He screams:

MISTER SEÑOR LOVE DADDY

WAKE UP!

CUT TO:

109　**INT:** *TINA'S BEDROOM—DAY*

Mookie jumps out of her bed; Tina sleeps by his side and their son
Hector is between them.

MISTER SEÑOR LOVE DADDY (VO)

WAKE UP!

MOOKIE

Fuck! My money!

TINA

Where are you going?

MOOKIE

To get my money.

TINA

Mookie, you must think I'm stupid
or something. You're gonna run
outta here and I won't see your
black ass for another week.

MOOKIE

Tina, it's not like that.

Mookie is putting on his clothes.

TINA

You don't care about me and you
definately don't care 'bout
your son.

MOOKIE

Tina, I'll be right back.

TINA

Be a man.

MOOKIE

I am a man.

TINA

Act like one then. Be a man.

MOOKIE

Later.

TINA

You're to the curb. You better
step off. Get a life.

Mookie leaves.

109A   MOTHER SISTER'S BEDROOM—DAY

Da Mayor wakes up in Mother Sister's big brass bed (she was born
in it). At first he has no idea where he's at, then sees Mother Sister
sitting down across the room smiling at him.

MOTHER SISTER

Good morning.

DA MAYOR

Is it a good morning?

MOTHER SISTER

Yes indeed. You almost got yourself
killed last night.

DA MAYOR

I've done that before.

Da Mayor gets up out of her big brass bed.

DA MAYOR

Where did you sleep?

MOTHER SISTER

I didn't.

DA MAYOR

I hope the block is still standing.

MOTHER SISTER

We're still standing.

Da Mayor and Mother Sister both look out the parlor window to see THE BLOCK and Mookie.

110 **EXT:** *SAL'S FAMOUS PIZZERIA—DAY*

Mookie walks up to Sal's Famous Pizzeria as it still smoulders in the morning light. Sal emerges from the wreckage; he looks like he might have slept there.

SAL

Whatdafuck do you want?

MOOKIE

I wants my money. I wants to
get paid.

Sal looks at Mookie in disbelief.

SAL

Mookie, I always liked you.
Not the smartest kid, but
you're honest. Don't make
me dislike you.

MOOKIE

Sal, I want my money.

SAL

Don't even ask about your
money. Your money wouldn't
even pay for that window you
smashed.

MOOKIE

Motherfuck a window, Radio Raheem
is dead.

SAL

You're right, a kid is dead, but
Mook, this isn't the time.

MOOKIE

Fuck dat. The time is fuckin'
now. Y'know I'm sorry 'bout
Sal's Famous Pizzeria, but I
gotta live, too. I gotta get
paid.

SAL

We both do.

MOOKIE

We all know you're gonna get
over with the insurance money
anyway! Ya know da deal.

SAL

Do we now?

MOOKIE

Quit bullshitting.

SAL

You don't know shit about shit.

MOOKIE

I know I wants to get my money.

Sal has had it.

SAL

How much? How much do I owe
you?

MOOKIE

My salary. Two-fifty.

Sal pulls out a wad and quickly peels off hundred dollar bills.

SAL

One, two, three, four, five.

Sal throws the "C" notes at Mookie, they hit him in the chest and
fall to the sidewalk.

SAL

Are you happy now? That's
five fucking hundred dollars.
You just got paid. Mookie, you
are a rich man, now ya life is
set, you'll never have another
worry, a care in the world.
Mookie, ya wealthy, a fuckin'
Rockefeller.

Mookie is stunned by Sal's outburst. He picks up the bills.

SAL

Ya just got paid, so leave me
the fuck alone.

MOOKIE

You only pay me two-fifty a week.
(he throws two "C" notes back at him)
I owe you fifty bucks.

SAL

Keep it.

MOOKIE

You keep it.

SAL

Christmas came early.

Both look at the two hundred-dollar bills on the sidewalk and refuse
to pick them up. It's a stalemate.

MOOKIE

This is the hottest Christmas
I've known.

Mookie counts his money.

SAL

It's supposed to be even hotter
today.

MOOKIE

You gonna open up another
Sal's Famous Pizzeria?

SAL

No. What are you gonna do?

MOOKIE

Make dat money. Get paid.

SAL

Yeah! . . . I'm goin' to the
beach for the first day in
fifteen years. Gonna take
the day off and go to the
beach.

MOOKIE

I can dig it. It's gonna be
HOT as a motherfucker.

SAL

Mookie?

> **MOOKIE**
> Gotta go.

> **SAL**
> C'mere, Doctor.

Mookie turns around and goes back.

> **SAL**
> Doctor, this is Sal talkin'.

> **MOOKIE**
> OK. OK.

> **SAL**
> Doctor, always try to do the
> right thing.

> **MOOKIE**
> That's it?

> **SAL**
> That's it.

Mookie thinks about it, looks at the two "C" notes still smiling up at him. He quickly scoops them up.

> **MOOKIE**
> I got it.

111 **EXT:** *STREET—DAY*

HIGH ANGLE

As Mookie turns and walks away, Sal goes back into Sal's Famous Pizzeria to salvage what is salvageable, and The Block begins to awake from its slumber, ready to deal once again with the heat of the hottest day of the year.

FADE OUT.

ROLL CREDITS.

STORYBOARDS

A storyboard is a visual guide to each shot—what it will look like on screen, how it will cut together with other shots in the film. *Do The Right Thing* is the first film for which I've used such detailed storyboards. The riot sequence was too big, too involved, and too costly to allow for the time it takes to design shots at the spur of the moment on the set. About a month before we filmed the sequence, I sat down with Ernest Dickerson, who created the shot list for the riot, and Jeff Balsmeyer, the storyboard artist, and went over the sequence shot by shot. Balsmeyer did the rest. What follows are the boards of scenes 92 and 93.

SCENE (92) P. 78

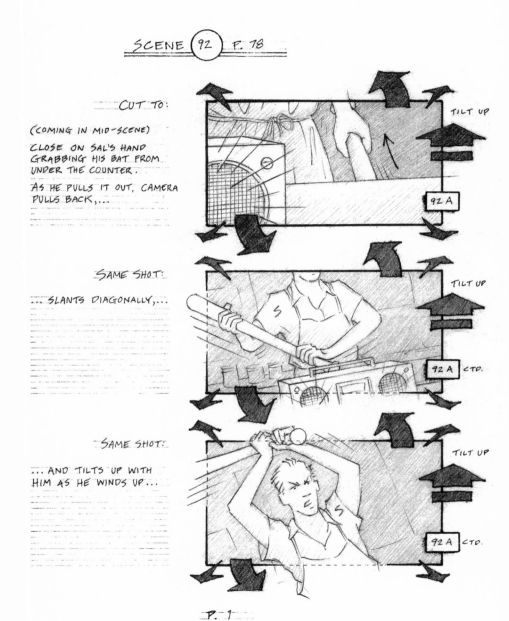

CUT TO:

(COMING IN MID-SCENE)

CLOSE ON SAL'S HAND GRABBING HIS BAT FROM UNDER THE COUNTER.

AS HE PULLS IT OUT, CAMERA PULLS BACK,...

TILT UP

92 A

SAME SHOT:

... SLANTS DIAGONALLY,...

TILT UP

92 A <TD.

SAME SHOT:

... AND TILTS UP WITH HIM AS HE WINDS UP...

TILT UP

92 A <TD.

P. 1

SCENE (92) P. 78

SAME SHOT:

...AND SWINGS DOWN OUT
OF FRAME.

92A CTD.

CUT TO:

CLOSE ON RADIO RAHEEM'S
BOX AS THE BAT SMASHES
DOWN.

THE MUSIC STOPS.

92B

CUT TO:

RADIO RAHEEM - REACTION.

92C

P. 2

SCENE (92) P. 78

BACK TO:

THE BOX.
SAL SWINGS AGAIN AND
AGAIN, SMASHING IT
TO SMITHEREENS.

92 B CTD.

CUT TO:

MOOKIE — REACTION.

92 D

CUT TO:

VITO AND PINO —
REACTION.

92 E

P. 3

SCENE (92) P. 78

CUT TO:

BUGGIN' OUT — REACTION.

CUT TO:

AHMAD, CEE, PUNCHY,
AND ELLA — REACTION.

CUT TO:

SMILEY — REACTION.

(COVER HIM CRAWLING
  UNDER A BOOTH.)

P. 4

SCENE (93) P. 80

CUT TO:

BUGGIN' OUT'S POV —
PUSHING IN AS OFFICER
LONG PUTS A CHOKE HOLD
ON RADIO RAHEEM TO RE-
STRAIN HIM.

93 N

SAME SHOT:

RADIO RAHEEM STILL
STRUGGLES, AND LONG
PULLS BACK HARD.

93 N CTD.

CUT TO:

LOWER ANGLE ON RADIO
RAHEEM'S FEET, WHICH
LIFT UP OFF THE GROUND.

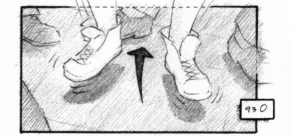

93 O

P. 76

SCENE (93) P. 80

BACK TO:

HIGHER ANGLE - RADIO
RAHEEM STOPS STRUG-
GLING ALTOGETHER, ...

93 N CTD.

SAME SHOT:

... HIS BODY GOES LIMP,
AND HE FALLS OUT OF
FRAME.

BACK TO:

LOWER ANGLE - HE DROPS
TO THE GROUND LIKE A
SACK OF POTATOES.

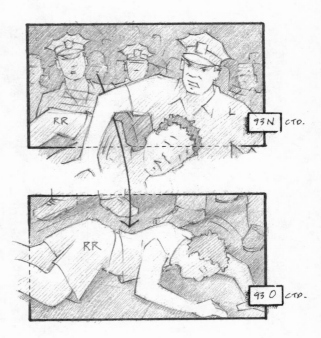

93 N CTD.

93 O CTD.

P. 17

SCENE 93 P. 80

BACK TO:

HIGHER ANGLE — THE
COPS LOOK DOWN, BEGIN
TO KICK HIM.
LONG: "GET UP! GET UP!

93 N | CTO.

BACK TO:

LOWER ANGLE — THE
COP'S FEET KICK RADIO
RAHEEM, WHO JUST LIES
THERE LIKE A BUMB ON
A LOG.
L(OS): "QUIT FAKING.

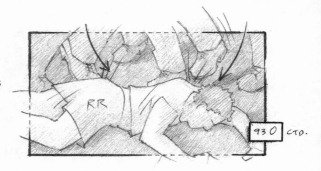

93 O | CTO.

BACK TO:

REVERSE, LOW ANGLE
OVER COP'S FEET KICK-
ING RADIO RAHEEM'S
BODY.
IN THE BG — THE CROWD.

93 L | CTO.

P. 18

SCENE 93 P. 80

BACK TO:

HIGHER ANGLE — THE
OFFICERS ALL LOOK AT
EACH OTHER. THEY
KNOW EXACTLY WHAT
THEY'VE DONE.
PONTE: "LET'S GET HIM
OUTTA HERE."
THEY DUCK DOWN.

93 N CTD.

CUT TO:

REVERSE, HAND-HELD,
FOLLOWING THE COPS AS
THEY LIFT UP RADIO
RAHEEM'S LIMP BODY...

93 P

HAND-HELD

SAME SHOT:

... AND CARRY IT
THROUGH THE CROWD...

93 P CTD.

HAND-HELD

P. 19

SCENE (93) P. 82

BACK TO:

MOOKIE TURNS AND
WALKS AWAY.

VOICE (TO MAYOR):
"YEAH, YOU!

BACK TO:

HIGH ANGLE ON DA MAYOR
AND SAL & SONS.

DM: "IF WE DON'T STOP
THIS NOW WE'LL ALL
REGRET IT... SAL AND
HIS TWO SONS HAD
NOTHING TO DO WITH
WHAT THE POLICE DID.

BACK TO:

CROWD.

VOICE: "GET OUT OF THE
WAY, OLD MAN.
YOU A TOM ANY-
WAY.

P. 26

SCENE (93) P. 82

BACK TO:

HIGH WIDE ANGLE.
DM: "LET 'EM BE.

93 T CTD.

CUT TO:

ANGLE ACROSS THE
STREET ON MOOKIE
DUMPING OUT A GARBAGE
CAN.

CRANE BACK AHEAD OF
HIM AS HE...

93 V

SAME SHOT:

... RUNS WITH THE CAN...

93 V CTD.

CRANE

P. 27

SCENE 93 P. 82

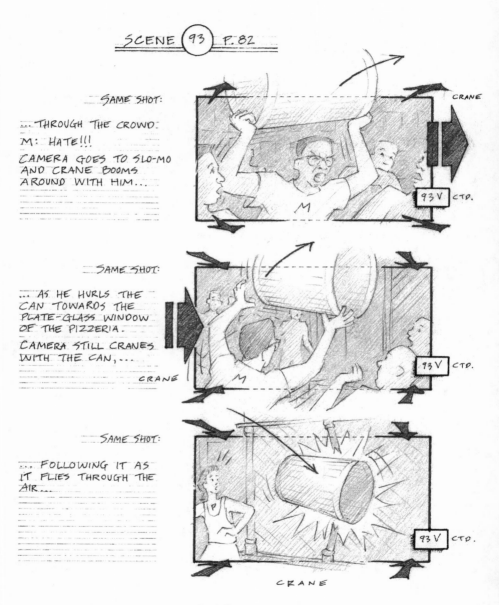

SAME SHOT:

...THROUGH THE CROWD.
M: HATE!!!
CAMERA GOES TO SLO-MO
AND CRANE BOOMS
AROUND WITH HIM...

CRANE

93 V CTD.

SAME SHOT:

... AS HE HURLS THE
CAN TOWARDS THE
PLATE-GLASS WINDOW
OF THE PIZZERIA.
CAMERA STILL CRANES
WITH THE CAN,...

CRANE

93 V CTD.

SAME SHOT:

... FOLLOWING IT AS
IT FLIES THROUGH THE
AIR...

93 V CTD.

CRANE

P. 28

SCENE 93 P. 82

— SAME SHOT:

... AND SMASHES
THROUGH THE GLASS.

93 V CTD.

OR, AN ALTERNATE VERSION OF THE GARBAGE CAN TOSS:

CUT TO:

MOOKIE DUMPS OUT THE
GARBAGE CAN.

CRANE BACK AHEAD OF
HIM...

93 V

P. 29

EPILOGUE

I t's one of the coldest days in December, seven months until we release the film. Y'know, some things you get a feeling about. A feeling deep down inside of you, a feeling that something special, something magical is gonna happen. Well, I've had this feeling from the git-go about *Do The Right Thing*. I may be wrong, but I always trust my instincts.

The idea came to me a year ago, and now we're in the final stages of postproduction. It's all coming together. Last week we recorded the score featuring the Branford Marsalis sextet backed by a forty-eight-piece string section. It's definitely my father, Bill Lee's, best.

Two weeks ago I flew out to Los Angeles to show the big cheeses at Universal a rough cut of the film. When the lights came up at the end of the screening, the studio brass just sat there in silence, almost stupefied. The silence went on for what seemed like an eternity. Finally I asked Tom Pollock, president of Universal, "So are we gonna get a release?" Everyone started to laugh, the ice had been broken.

Universal's main concern, just like Paramount's, was the ending. Was it too open-ended? How would audiences feel leaving the theater? Will Blacks want to go on a rampage? Will whites feel uncomfortable? Here are some of the suggestions for alternative endings that were tossed around (at least those I listened to):

1. Mookie shouldn't pick up the money that Sal throws on the ground.

2. Put Mister Señor Love Daddy's "can we live together" speech at the very end of the film.

3. Shoot an epilogue with Mookie talking into the camera. (This was my idea.)

Flying back to Nueva York, I thought about these endings, but none felt right. Smiley's postcard, that photograph of Malcolm X and Martin Luther King shaking hands, kept coming back to me. I had to find a way to tie these two great men into the finale.

King and Malcolm. Both men died for the love of their people, but had different strategies for realizing freedom. Why not end the film with an appropriate quote from each? In the end, justice will prevail one way or another. There are two paths to that. The way of King, or the way of Malcolm.

Am I advocating violence? No, but goddamn, the days of twenty-five million Blacks being silent while our fellow brothers and sisters are exploited, oppressed, and murdered, have to come to an end. Racial persecution, not only in the United States, but all over the world, is not gonna go away; it seems it's getting worse (four years of Bush won't help). And if Crazy Eddie Koch gets reelected for a fourth term as mayor of New York, what you see in *Do The Right Thing* will be light stuff. Yep, we have a choice, Malcolm or King. I know who I'm down with.

Spike Lee
December 17, 1988
Brooklyn, New York
By Any Means Necessary
Ya Dig Sho-Nuff

SPIKE LEE JOINTOGRAPHY

FEATURE FILMS

She's Gotta Have It—1986
School Daze—1988
Do The Right Thing—1989

MUSIC VIDEOS

She's Gotta Have It—1986
Miles Davis—1986
Branford Marsalis—1986
Anita Baker—1987
EU—*School Daze*—1988
Keith John—*School Daze*—1988
Phyllis Hyman—*School Daze*—1988
The Rays—*School Daze*—1988
Steel Pulse—1988
EU—Buck Wild—1989
Public Enemy—*Do The Right Thing*—1989
Guy - *Do The Right Thing*—1989
Perri - *Do The Right Thing*—1989

SHORT FILMS

Five one-minute spots—MTV—1986
Horn of Plenty—Saturday Night Live—1986

STUDENT FILMS (NEW YORK UNIVERSITY)

The Answer—1980
Sarah—1981
Joe's Bed-Stuy Barbershop: We Cut Heads—1982

COMMERCIALS

Air Jordan (Hang Time), Nike—1988
Air Jordan (Cover), Nike—1988
Jesse Jackson,
New York Democratic Primary campaign spot—1988
Air Jordan (Rappin'), Nike—1989
Air Jordan (Can/Can't), Nike—1989
Air Jordan (Nola), Nike—1989

BOOKS

Spike Lee's Gotta Have It: Inside Guerrilla Filmmaking—1987
Uplift the Race: The Construction of School Daze—1988
Do The Right Thing: A Spike Lee Joint—1989

DO THE RIGHT THING
Fight the Power
A Forty Acres and a Mule Filmworks Production

YA-DIG   SHO-NUFF
BY ANY MEANS NECESSARY

MPAA Rating—R   Running Time—1:59

DO THE RIGHT THING
CREDITS

CAST

Sal	*Danny Aiello*
Da Mayor	*Ossie Davis*
Mother Sister	*Ruby Dee*
Vito	*Richard Edson*
Buggin' Out	*Giancarlo Esposito*
Mookie	*Spike Lee*
Radio Raheem	*Bill Nunn*
Pino	*John Turturro*
ML	*Paul Benjamin*
Coconut Sid	*Frankie Faison*
Sweet Dick Willie	*Robin Harris*
Jade	*Joie Lee*
Officer Ponte	*Miguel Sandoval*
Officer Long	*Rick Aiello*
Clifton	*John Savage*
Mister Señor Love Daddy	*Sam Jackson*
Tina	*Rosie Perez*
Smiley	*Roger Guenveur Smith*
Ahmad	*Steve White*
Cee	*Martin Lawrence*
Punchy	*Leonard Thomas*
Ella	*Christa Rivers*
Charlie	*Frank Vincent*
Stevie	*Luis Ramos*
Eddie	*Richard Habersham*
Louise	*Gwen McGee*
Sonny	*Steve Park*
Kim	*Ginny Yang*
Korean Child	*Sherwin Park*
Puerto Rican Icee Man	*Shawn Elliott*
Carmen	*Diva Osorio*
Stevie's Friends	*Chris Delaney*
	Angel Ramirez
	Sixto Ramos
	Nelson Vasquez

Hector	*Travell Lee Toulson*
Sergeant	*Joel Nagle*
Plainclothes Detective	*David E. Weinberg*
Double Dutch Girls	*Yattee Brown*
	Mecca Brunson
	Shawn Stainback
	Soquana Wallace
Stunt Double (Sal)	*Danny Aiello, Jr.*
Stunt Driver	*Mharaka Washington*
Stunt Players	*Gary Frith*
	Andy Duppin
	Rashon Khan
	Erik Koniger
	Malcolm Livingston
	David S. Lomax
	Dominic Marcus
	Eric A. Payne
	Roy Thomas
	Tom Wright

FILMMAKERS

Produced, Written, and Directed by	Spike Lee
Coproducer	Monty Ross
Line Producer	Jon Kilik
Photographed by	Ernest Dickerson
Editor	Barry Alexander Brown
Original Music Score	Bill Lee
Production Design	Wynn Thomas
Casting	Robi Reed
Costumes	Ruthe Carter
Sound Design	Skip Lievsay
Production Supervisor	Preston Holmes
1st Assistant Director	Randy Fletcher
2nd Assistant Director	Nandi Bowe
2nd 2nd Assistant Director	Chris Lopez
Location Manager	Brent Owens
Unit Manager	R.W. Dixon
Production Office Coordinator	Lillian Pyles
Assistant Production Office Coordinator	Robin Downes
Forty Acres Production Coordinator	Susan D. Fowler
Forty Acres Production Assistant	Audra C. Smith
Production Comptroller	Robert Nickson
Auditor	Holly Chase
Assistant Auditor	Eric Oden
Script Supervisor	Joe Gonzalez
Camera Operator	John Newby
1st Assistant Camera	Jonathan Burkhart
2nd Assistant Camera	Darnell Martin
Additional Camera Operators	Frank Prinzi
	George Pattison
Additional Camera Assistants	Robert Gorelick
	Paul S. Reuter
Louma Crane Technician	Stuart Allen
Still Photography	David Lee
Assistant Art Director	Michael Green
	Dennis Bradford
Art Department Coordinator	Pam Stephens

Storyboard Artist	*Jeff Balsmeyer*
Chargeman	*Jeffrey L. Glave*
2nd Scenic Artist	*Joyce Kubalak*
Scenic Artists	*Patricia Bases*
	Lawrence Casey
	Jeff Miller
Property Master	*Octavio Molina*
1st Assistant Props	*Mark Selemon*
2nd Assistant Props	*Marc Henry Johnson*
3rd Assistant Props	*Kevin Ladson*
Additional Assistant Props	*Andy Lassman*
Leadman	*Scott Rosenstock*
Key Set Dresser	*Keith Wall*
Set Decorator	*Steve Rosse*
Assistant Set Decorator	*Jon Rudo*
Set Dressers	*Anthony Baldasare*
	Michael Lee Benson
	James Bilz
	Thomas Hudson Reeve
Shop Person	*Rosalie Russino*
Production Assistant—Shop	*Sherman Benjamin*
Construction Coordinator	*Martin Bernstein*
Construction Grips	*James Bonice*
	David Bromberg
	Jonathan Graham
	Rich Kerekes
	Charles Marroquin
	Monique Mitchell
	Carl Peterson
	Carl Prinzi
	Bryan Unger
Production Assistant—Construction	*Robert Woods, Jr.*
Key Set Builder	*Ken Nelson*
Carpenters	*Rodney Clark*
	Dominic Ferrar
	Harold Horn
	Timothy Main
	Chris Miller
	Twad Schuetrum
Key Grip	*Robert Ippolito*
Best Boy	*Paul Wachter*

Dolly Grip	*Rex North*
3rd Grip	*Rodney Bauer*
Additional Grips	*John Archibald*
	Erich Augenstein
	Donald Bailer
	Roger Kimpton
Grip Trainee	*Marcus Turner*
Gaffer	*Charles Houston*
Best Boy	*Val DeSalvo*
3rd Electrics	*Sergei Mihajlov*
	John O'Malley
Generator Operator	*Derrick Still*
Electrics	*James Boorman*
	Christopher Vanzant
Electric Trainees	*Addison Cook*
	Juan Lopez
Production Assistant—Electric	*Beverly C. Jones*
Assistant Editor	*Tula Goenka*
Apprentice Editor	*Leander Sales*
Supervising Dialogue Editor	*Philip Stockton*
Dialogue Editor	*Jeff Stern*
ADR Editor	*Brunilda Torres*
Music Editor	*Alex Steyermark*
Foley Editor	*Gail Showalter*
Sound Editors	*Rudy Gaskins*
	Gene Gearty
	Tony Martinez
	Bruce Pross
	Stuart Stanley
Assistant Sound Editors	*James Flatto*
	Marissa Littlefield
	Nic Ratner
Apprentice Sound Editors	*Nzingha Clarke*
	William Docker
Foley Artist	*Marko A. Costanzo*
Re-Recording Mixer	*Tom Fleischman*
Mixed at	*Sound One Studios*
Dailies Projection	*Boston Light and Sound*
Projectionist (Dailies)	*Michael Gaynor*
Dolby Stereo Consultant	*Mike Di Cosimo*
Music Copyist	*James "Jabbo" Ware*

Piano Tuner	*Alexander Ostrovsky*
"Fight the Power" Choreography	*Rosie Perez*
	Otis Sallid
Special Effects	*Steve Kirshoff*
Assistant Effects	*John N. Berry*
	Wilfred Caban
	Paul Collangello
	Dave Fletcher
	Bill Harrison
	Don Hewitt
	William Van Der Putten
	Dennis Zack
Assistant Costume Designer	*Karen Perry*
Wardrobe Supervisor	*Jennifer Ruscoe*
Wardrobe Seamstress	*Valerie A. Gladstone*
Production Assistants—Wardrobe	*Michele Boissiere*
	Millicent Shelton
Hair	*Larry Cherry*
Makeup	*Matiki Anoff*
Additional Makeup	*Marianna Najjar*
Casting Assistant	*Andrea Reed*
Extras Casting	*Sarah Hyde-Hamlet*
Production Assistant—Casting	*Tracy Vilar*
Stunt Coordinator	*Eddie Smith*
Stunt Coordinator Assistants	*Chantal Collins*
	Francine Renee Lawrence
Teamster Captain	*Jim Leavey*
Drivers	*Willi Gaskins*
	Clifford Johnson
	Sullie Jordan
	Brian Maxwell
	Martin Whitfield
	Carlos Williams
Production Assistants—Set	*Kenny Buford*
	Spencer Charles
	Eric Daniel
	Michael Ellis
	Eddie Joe
	Stephanie Jones
	Erik Night
	Frederick Nielsen

	Kia Puriefoy
	Bruce Roberts
	Dale Watkins
Production Assistants—Office	*Steve Burnett*
	Judith Norman
Interns	*Richard Beaumont*
	Kai Bowe
	Dawn Cain
	Fritz Celestin
	Melissa A. Clark
	Arlene Donnelly
	Juliette Harris
	Ernie Mapp
	Mitchell Marchand
	Jacki Newson
	Traci Proctor
	Sara Renaud
	Carolyn Rouse
	Astrid Roy
	Sharoya N. Smalls
	Alan C. Smith
	Susan Stuart
	Karen Taylor
	Jean Warner
	Latanya White
	Gail White
	Monique Williams
Emergency Medical Services	*On Location Medical, Inc.*
Legal Services	*Frankfurt, Garbus, Klein and Selz*
Completion Guarantee	*The Completion Bond Company*
Publicity	*Tobin and Associates*
Unit Publicist	*Sam Mattingly*
Caterers	*T & A Caterers*
	Central Falls Caterers
Product Placement	*Unique Product Placement*
	Norm Marshall & Associates, Inc.
Product Placement Coordinator	*Avril Lacour-Hartnagel*
Craft Services	*Cheryl Ann Scott*

Camera Equipment	*Technological Cinevideo Services, Inc.*
Sound Equipment	*Audio Services*
Negative Matching	*Noëlle Pinraat*
Opticals	*Select Effects*
Photo Research	*The Schomburg Center for Research in Black Culture*
	New York Public Library
Malcolm X/Martin Luther King, Jr. Photos Courtesy of	*World Wide Photos/ Peggy Farrell*
Main and End Titles designed and produced by	*Balsmeyer and Everett, Inc.*
Do The Right Thing Logo by	*Art Sims/11:24 Design & Advertising*
Music Score recorded at	*RCA Studios, N.Y.*
Color by	*Du Art Laboratories, Inc.*
Prints by	*Deluxe®*

THE MUSIC

"Fight the Power"
Music and lyrics by Carlton Ridenhour, Hank Shocklee, Eric Sadler, and
    Keith Shocklee
Performed by PUBLIC ENEMY
Def American Songs, Inc. (BMI)
Courtesy of DefJam / CBS Records

"Don't Shoot Me"
Music and lyrics by Spike Lee, Mervyn Warren, Claude McKnight, and
    David Thomas
Performed by TAKE 6
Spikey-Poo Songs, Inc. (ASCAP)/Dee Mee Music/Mervyn Warren Music/
    Claude Vee Music (BMI)
Courtesy of Reprise/Warner Brothers Records

"Can't Stand It"
Music and lyrics by David Hines
Performed by STEEL PULSE
Pulse Music, Ltd. (P.R.S.)
Courtesy of MCA Records

"Tú y Yo"
Music and lyrics by Rubèn Blades
Performed by RUBÈN BLADES
R. B. Productions, Inc. (ASCAP)
Courtesy of Elektra Records

"Why Don't We Try"
Music and lyrics by Raymond Jones, Larry DeCarmine, Vincent Morris
Performed by KEITH JOHN
Jerrelle Music Publishing (ASCAP)
Zubaidah Music, Inc./Unicity Music Publishing (ASCAP)
Hey Nineteen Music (ASCAP)
Courtesy of Black Bull Productions

"Hard to Say"
Music and lyrics by Raymond Jones
Performed by LORI PERRY and GERALD ALSTON

Zubaidah Music, Inc. (ASCAP)
Courtesy of Motown Records

"Party Hearty"
Music and lyrics by William "Ju Ju" House and Kent Wood
Performed by EU
Ju House Music (ASCAP) and Syce-M-Up Music (ASCAP)
Courtesy of Virgin Records

"Prove to Me"
Music and lyrics by Raymond Jones and Sami McKinney
Performed by PERRI
Zubaidah Music, Inc. (ASCAP), Unicity Music, Avid One Music (ASCAP)
Courtesy of Zebra/MCA Records

"Feel So Good"
Music and lyrics by Sami McKinney, Lori Perry, and Michael O'Hara
Performed by PERRI
O'Hara Music/Texas City Music (BMI), AVID One Music (ASCAP)
MCA Publishing/Perrylane Music (BMI)
Courtesy of Zebra/MCA Records

"My Fantasy"
Music and lyrics by Teddy Riley
Performed by Teddy Riley featuring GUY
Cal-Gene Music, Inc., Virgin Songs, Inc. (BMI)
Courtesy of MCA Records

"Never Explain Love"
Cathy Block lyrics by Raymond Jones and
Performed by AL JARREAU
Building Block Music (BMI)
Zubaidah Music Inc./Unicity Music Publishing (ASCAP)

WE LOVE RADIO Jingles
Writtten and performed by TAKE 6
Courtesy of Reprise/Warner Brothers Records

"Lift Every Voice and Sing"
Music and lyrics by James Weldon Johnson and John Rosemond Johnson

THE NATURAL SPIRITUAL ORCHESTRA

CONDUCTOR
William J.E. Lee

FEATURING
Branford Marsalis—Tenor and Soprano Saxophone

Terrence Blanchard—Trumpet
Marlon Jordan—Trumpet
Donald Harris—Alto Saxophone
Jeff "Train" Watts—Drums
Robert Hurst—Bass
Kenny Barron—Piano
James Williams—Piano

VIOLINS
Stanley G. Hunte—Contractor
Alen W. Sanford—Concert Master
Elliot Rosoff
Kenneth Gordon
John Pintavalle
Gerald Tarack
Charles Libove
Louann Motesi
Paul Peabody
Lewis Eley
Regis Iandiorio
Sandra Billingslea
Cecelia A. Hobbs
Marion J. Pinheiro
Richard Henrickson
Joseph Malin
Lesa Terry
Laura J. Smith
Diane Monroe
Alvin E. Rodgers
Elena Barere
Patmore Lewis
Gregory Komar
Winterton Garvey

VIOLAS
Alfred V. Brown
Harry Zaratzian
Barry Finclair
Maxine Roach
John R. Dexter
Lois E. Martin
Maureen Gallagher
Juliette Hassner

CELLOS
Frederick Zlotkin
Mark Orrin Shuman
Bruce Rogers
Melissa Meel
Eileen M. Folsom
Zela Terry
Carol Buck
Astrid Schween

BASS
Michael M. Fleming
Rufus Reid

Quotation by Malcolm X used by permission of Dr. Betty Shabazz

Quotation by Dr. Martin Luther King, Jr., used by permission of Mrs.
  Coretta Scott King

SPECIAL THANKS TO
Explosives Unit—New York City Fire Department
Orangetown Fire Company #1, South Nyack, N.Y.
John Wilson
Rush
New York City Board of Education and District 16
Public School #308
Antioch Baptist Church
Bed-Stuy Community Board #3

THANKS ALSO TO
BROOKLYN BEER
CANAL JEANS
ELAN JEWELRY
EL DIARIO/LA PRENSA
ELLIS COLLECTION
ESSENCE MAGAZINE
GITANO
JOHNSON PUBLICATIONS
LEVI STRAUSS & CO.
MR. SOFTEE, INC.
NIKE
NEW YORK DAILY NEWS
NEW YORK NEWSDAY
NEW YORK POST
NEW YORK TIMES COMPANY
OLD ENGLISH
PEPSI-COLA
RAY-BAN/BAUSCH & LOMB
WILLI WEAR
XENOBIA

New York City Mayor's Office for Film, Theatre, and Broadcasting
Shot on location in Bedford-Stuyvesant in the Great Borough of Brooklyn,
  New York